Non-Designer's Illustrator Book

The Non-Designer's Illustrator Book

Essential
vector
techniques
for design

Robin Williams & John Tollett

Peachpit Press
Berkeley
California

The Non-Designer's Illustrator Book
ROBIN WILLIAMS AND JOHN TOLLETT

©2012 by Robin Williams and John Tollett

Peachpit Press
1249 Eighth Street
Berkeley, California 94710
510.524.2178   voice
510.524.2221   fax

Editor:	Nikki McDonald
Proofer:	Cathy Lane
Interior design and production:	Robin Williams and John Tollett
Cover design and production:	John Tollett
Index:	Robin Williams
Prepress:	David Van Ness

Peachpit Press is a division of Pearson Education.

Find us on the web at www.peachpit.com.

To report errors, please send a note to errata@peachpit.com.

ISBN 13:   978-0-321-77287-9

ISBN 10:   0-321-77287-3

10 9 8 7 6 5 4 3 2 1

Printed and bound in the United States of America

Contents

SECTION 4   Manipulate Objects

Backmatter

Introduction

Creating professional illustration is within your grasp, whether that is a goal in your life or not. By the time you finish this book, you'll realize how remarkably easy it is to create professional-level art and design with Adobe Illustrator.

However, Illustrator is not just for professional artists, but for anyone who wants to create incredible graphics and design, at any level of expertise. Even a basic knowledge of Illustrator is enough to elevate your design and illustration skills to the next level.

Our focus in this book is on print, although creating art in Illustrator is the same whether your project is destined to be printed, put on a web page, or incorporated into a video project.

By the time you finish all of the tasks in this book, you won't know *everything* about Adobe Illustrator, but you'll know enough to surprise yourself with the work you produce. And truthfully, 90 percent of our projects require nothing more than what's in this book.

Enjoy the empowerment and inspiration that Adobe Illustrator provides, and Happy Vector Paths to you!

John

Everything I know about Illustrator I learned from John. He's amazing and I'm lucky. ♡

Robin

Section 1
The Very Basics

Trinity Church in Copley Square, Boston

Now that you have in your possession the most powerful vector illustration program in the history of mankind, you must use it wisely. Start by reading this first section, full of ancient wisdom that will help guide you the rest of your days. Or at least until you finish the tasks included in this book.

On the previous page: A sketch by John Tollett, drawn in a notebook while sitting in Copley Square, then traced using Live Trace (Chapter 8) as a piece of vector art that can be enlarged as big as a skyscraper.

Below is the outline version (the vector paths) of the traced image.

Trinity Church in Copley Square, Boston

1 Before You Begin

I know, I know—you want to jump right in and start creating amazing things! But first take just a couple of minutes to read through this short chapter and set a few preferences that will make your drawing life easier.

What is vector-based illustration?

All computer images are either pixel-based (as in photos you work with in Photoshop) or vector-based.

Pixel-based images (often referred to as *raster* or *bitmap* images) are made of tiny blocks of color (pixels), created at a certain **resolution** (a specific number of pixels per inch). The resolution for an image that's destined for high quality output, such as a commercial printing press, is usually set to 300 pixels per inch (300 ppi). The resolution for an image that's destined for low-quality output, such as art on a web page, is usually set to 72 ppi (a common *screen* resolution).

When you enlarge a raster image, individual pixels are enlarged, creating pixelated, blocky edges in place of smooth edges. If you enlarge a raster image too much, the image quality degrades noticeably.

A **vector image** is a *mathematical description* of shapes, fill, colors, strokes, gradients, and blends. The mathematics behind a vector image means you can resize it *any amount* without degrading the quality at all.

Even though Illustrator is primarily a vector application, you can combine both vector and raster elements in your projects if necessary. However, be aware of possible resolution issues in the raster elements.

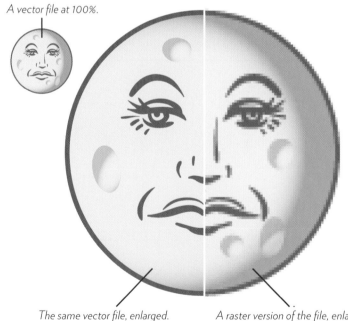

A vector file at 100%.

The same vector file, enlarged.   A raster version of the file, enlarged.

A few helpful settings before you start

Before you create a new document or start an illustration, modify some of your Illustrator settings to optimize your workflow, and so your settings will match ours as you follow along with the tasks in this book.

TASK 1 Adjust Illustrator's color settings

1 From the Edit menu, choose "Color Settings."

2 In the "Color Settings" dialog, make your settings match the ones shown below.

3 Click "Advanced Mode." In the "Conversion Options" section that appears, change the "Intent" pop-up menu to "Perceptual."

4 Click OK.

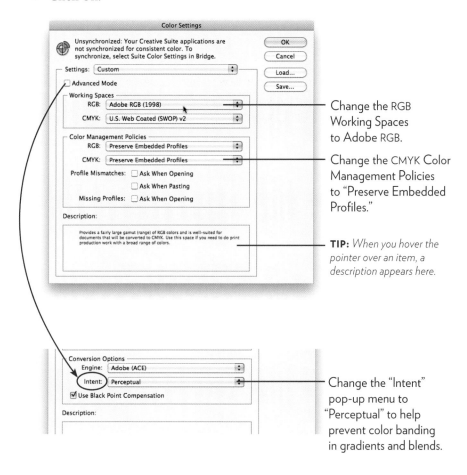

Change the RGB Working Spaces to Adobe RGB.

Change the CMYK Color Management Policies to "Preserve Embedded Profiles."

TIP: *When you hover the pointer over an item, a description appears here.*

Change the "Intent" pop-up menu to "Perceptual" to help prevent color banding in gradients and blends.

TIP: The "Working Spaces" RGB option called "Adobe RGB (1998)" provides a larger color range than the default "sRGB" option.

TASK 2   Change a few settings in Preferences

Illustrator's Preferences settings provide lots of options that allow you to work in a way that's most comfortable for you.

1   To open the Preferences dialog box, do one of the following:

- Mac: Choose Illustrator > Preferences > General.
  PC: Choose Edit > Preferences > General.

- If a document is open, with nothing selected, click the "Preferences" button in the Control panel across the top of the document window.

The most important *General* setting for now is **Keyboard Increment** (above). This value determines how far a selected object moves when you press the arrow keys on the keyboard. Enter a small number, as shown above, so you can make tiny adjustments when moving objects in your document.

2   From the Preferences pop-up menu, choose **Units**.

Set the "General" unit of measurement you prefer to be used in numerical entry fields and for settings in various panels.

For "Stroke" and "Type," choose "Points." This is the best unit with which to specify stroke and font sizes.

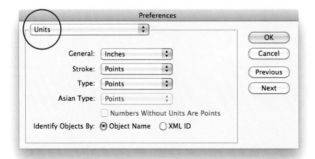

3   From the pop-up menu, choose **Selection & Anchor Display**.

Check the "Object Selection by Path Only" item.

With this option checked *on*, you must click on an object's path (its edge) to select it.

When this option is turned *off* (unchecked), you can select an object by clicking anywhere on its fill or on its edges. This, however, makes it difficult to select a path (or multiple paths) that's on top of or inside another object without accidently selecting the surrounding object. By thus limiting object selection to "Path Only," you can drag inside a shape to select other shapes, without selecting the shape you're dragging within (as long as the drag doesn't touch the *path* of the surrounding shape). Read more about *selections* in Chapter 2.

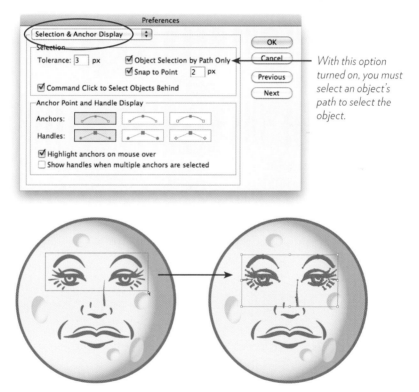

With this option turned on, you must select an object's path to select the object.

When the "Object Selection by Path Only" option is active, you can press-and-drag across the surface of objects without selecting them, such as the face of the moon.

The only objects selected, as shown above, are those whose paths are touched by the marquee selection shown on the left.

—continued

4   From the Preferences pop-up menu, choose **Appearance of Black**.

There are two types of black you can use in artwork: *pure black* (plain ol' 100% black ink) and *rich black* (100% black ink *plus* a percentage of the other three CMYK colors—cyan, magenta, and yellow, usually 20 percent of each). Rich black increases the black color's density and opacity. Rich black is used when a black color overprints other colors and you want the black to be opaque enough to prevent underlying colors from showing through.

a   From the "On Screen" pop-up menu, choose "Display All Blacks Accurately."

Pure black (100% black) actually appears on the screen as a very dark gray, and rich black appears as a dense, opaque black. Being able to see the difference can help you decide which black fills or strokes may need to be changed to a rich black color. If you were to choose the "Display All Blacks as Rich Black" option, all blacks will appear the same on-screen, but will output according to the "Printing/Exporting" option below.

b   From the "Printing/Exporting" pop-up menu, choose "Output All Blacks as Rich Black."

This setting affects documents printed to non-PostScript desktop printers and documents exported to an RGB file format, such as a JPEG image. If you choose the "Output All Blacks Accurately" option here, you'll be able to see the difference between pure blacks and rich blacks when you print to a non-PostScript desktop printer or export to an RGB file format.

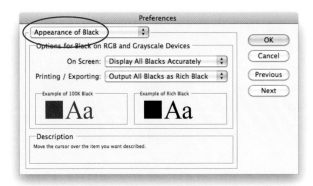

The Illustrator Preferences provide many other settings you can customize to your liking. Explore them all! Meanwhile, these settings will get you started.

2 Before You Draw

This chapter contains an overview of the workspace you'll be using, plus an explanation of many of the basic features and tools that are part of almost every project: how to create a new document, understanding artboards, using guides, how to switch screen modes, and more. Some of this information won't quite make sense to you until you start working on a project, but we want you to know it exists and where to find it when you need it.

Illustrator often provides several different ways to do a certain task, even such a basic one as creating a new document. The best method often depends on the task at hand or just a personal preference for how you like to work. We don't try to describe all of the various options in every case, so be aware that as you become more familiar with Illustrator, you may discover alternative techniques that you prefer. It's your job to explore!

Create a new document

To become familiar with your workspace and the panels that provide all the options for your drawing and painting tools, you first need to create a document. There are a couple of ways to do this. If you see the Welcome Screen (shown below) on your monitor when you open Illustrator, follow the directions in Task 1. If you do not see that screen, follow the directions in Task 2 to open a document from the File menu, as usual.

TASK 1   Use the Welcome Screen to create a new document

When you first open Illustrator, a Welcome Screen appears in which you can open *recent items* (projects you worked on earlier, listed on the left side) or **create a new document.**

1   On the right side of the Welcome pane, you see a list of the sorts of documents that you can create in Illustrator, under "Create New." Choose "Print Document." A "New Document" dialog box opens; see Step 2 on the opposite page.

To skip the "New Document" dialog box and open a document using whatever document settings are already set up, Option-click (PC: Alt-click) the "Print Document" option.

Feel free to open a template so there is something on your screen. *A template always opens a copy,* so you can't hurt anything.

TIP: To skip this Welcome Screen in the future, check this box (you can always open the Welcome Screen from the Help menu). If you decide you *do* want it to always appear, choose Help > Welcome Screen, then uncheck the "Don't show again" box.

TASK 2 Use the File menu to create a new document

1 Choose File > New….

2 In the "New Document" dialog box shown below, make the following
settings (most of the settings suggested here are not critical at this
point and can be modified later).

- You can name the document, but this does *not* save the file!
In fact, we recommend you leave this field "Untitled" to remind
you that you have not yet saved the file to your disk.

- Choose the "New Document Profile" called "Print." This
automatically sets the options shown below, with a letter-sized
board, CMYK color mode, and high-resolution raster effects.

- Set the "Number of Artboards" to 1.
Artboards are kind of like drawing boards. A single document
can have multiple artboards (up to 100, depending on size).
See pages 20–23 to learn important stuff about artboards.

- Click OK. A blank document window opens, ready for some
creative genius to start slinging vector paths and shapes around.
But remember to save your file with a name before you do much!

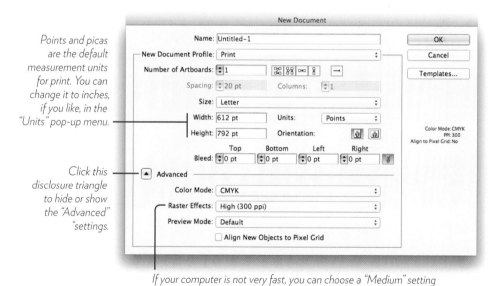

*Points and picas
are the default
measurement units
for print. You can
change it to inches,
if you like, in the
"Units" pop-up menu.*

*Click this
disclosure triangle
to hide or show
the "Advanced"
"settings.*

*If your computer is not very fast, you can choose a "Medium" setting
here so raster objects will display on your screen more quickly.*

1 inch = 72 points	**TIP:** You can change the document color
1 inch = 6 picas	mode at any time from CMYK to RGB:
1 pica = 12 points	Choose File > Document Color Mode > RGB Color.

11

Illustrator's workspace overview

When you open Illustrator, a default **workspace** fills the screen, as shown below. In the top-right (circled), you can see that the workspace shown below is "Essentials," a good place to start. Other preset workspaces include slightly different sets of panels, but you can customize the workspace to suit yourself.

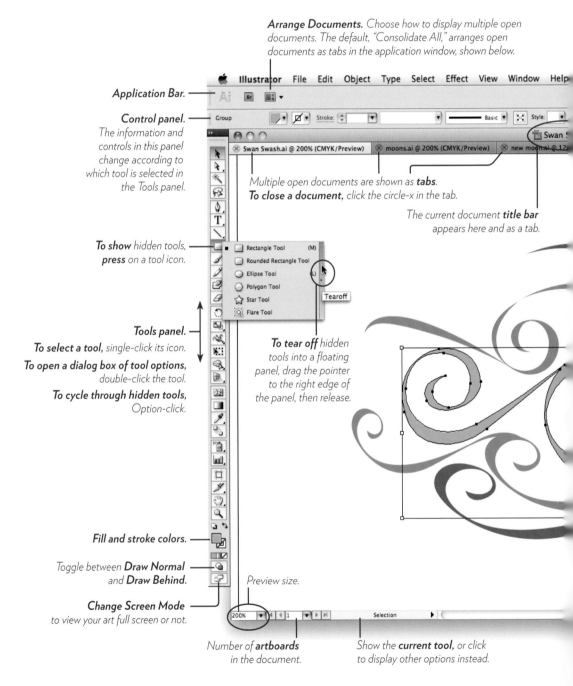

Arrange Documents. *Choose how to display multiple open documents. The default, "Consolidate All," arranges open documents as tabs in the application window, shown below.*

Application Bar.

Control panel.
The information and controls in this panel change according to which tool is selected in the Tools panel.

Multiple open documents are shown as **tabs.**
To close a document, *click the circle-x in the tab.*

The current document **title bar** *appears here and as a tab.*

To show *hidden tools,* **press** *on a tool icon.*

☐ Rectangle Tool	(M)
☐ Rounded Rectangle Tool	
○ Ellipse Tool	(L)
○ Polygon Tool	
☆ Star Tool	
▨ Flare Tool	

Tearoff

Tools panel.
To select a tool, *single-click its icon.*
To open a dialog box of tool options, *double-click the tool.*
To cycle through hidden tools, *Option-click.*

To tear off *hidden tools into a floating panel, drag the pointer to the right edge of the panel, then release.*

Fill and stroke colors.

Toggle between **Draw Normal** *and* **Draw Behind.**

Preview size.

Change Screen Mode *to view your art full screen or not.*

Number of **artboards** *in the document.*

Show the **current tool,** *or click to display other options instead.*

Add panels to the workspace

If a panel you want to use is not included in the current workspace, go to the Window menu and choose it. Panels that are *active* in the workspace (such as the Layers panel shown below) have checkmarks next to their names in the Window menu. Learn more about panels on the following pages.

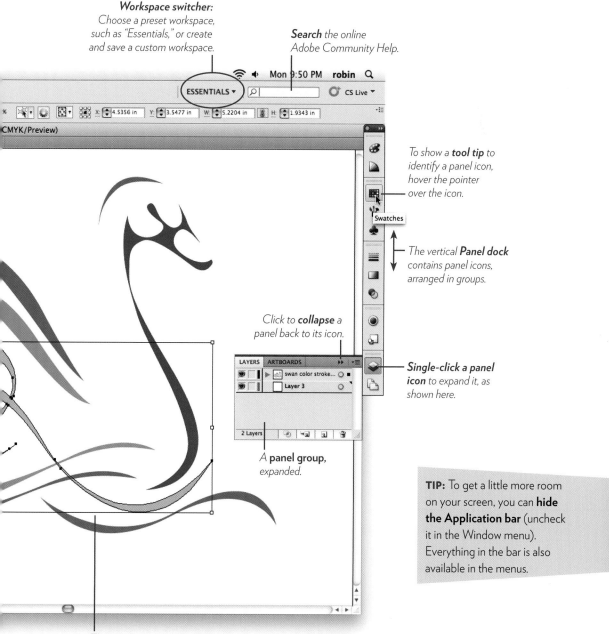

Workspace switcher:
Choose a preset workspace, such as "Essentials," or create and save a custom workspace.

Search the online Adobe Community Help.

To show a **tool tip** to identify a panel icon, hover the pointer over the icon.

The vertical **Panel dock** contains panel icons, arranged in groups.

Click to **collapse** a panel back to its icon.

Single-click a panel icon to expand it, as shown here.

A **panel group,** expanded.

TIP: To get a little more room on your screen, you can **hide the Application bar** (uncheck it in the Window menu). Everything in the bar is also available in the menus.

This art is made of **paths** drawn with the Pen tool. A selection box surrounds the object that is currently selected. Chapter 5 reveals the secrets of the Pen tool. Bwahahaha!

The Control panel (see the opposite page).

The Application bar

The Application bar at the top of the Illustrator window (shown below and on the previous pages) contains a couple of useful items.

Go to Bridge.   Arrange Documents.   Workspace Switcher.

The Bridge connection

Click the *Go to Bridge* icon to open the application called Bridge. We don't cover Bridge in this book because it's not essential to learning Illustrator, but keep in mind that it's a very useful tool that is closely integrated with all of the Adobe Creative suite applications. Bridge is a visual browser and file manager that lets you locate, preview, and organize files, plus much more. You can also get to Bridge from Illustrator's File menu.

The Arrange Documents menu

Click the *Arrange Documents* icon to open a panel of arrangement thumbnails. The thumbnails represent different ways to display multiple open documents. The default setting, "Consolidate All" (best in most situations), arranges open documents as tabs across the top of the document window.

The Workspace Switcher options

Click the *Workspace Switcher* icon to open a menu of workspace presets. Choose any preset, then rearrange the space as you work. For instance, you might choose the "Essentials" preset, then later add other panels to the workspace. **To save that customized workspace to use again later,** click the *Workspace Switcher* icon, then choose "Save Workspace...."

TIP: You can arrange documents as well as save and change workspaces from the Window menu.

The Control panel

The Control panel, shown above, sits on top of the document window. *The controls, input fields, pop-up menus, buttons, and options available in the Control panel change depending on the tool you're using.* Keep an eye on the Control panel because it almost always gives you fast and easy access to settings you need, without having to navigate through menus or panels to find the same thing. Once you start drawing, painting, or creating a design, you'll use this panel more than any other.

The Control panel menu

Click the small menu icon on the far-right side of the Control panel (shown circled) to open the **Control panel menu.** At the very top of the menu you can choose to have the Control panel docked to the top (its default position) or to the bottom of your window.

The menu also contains a list of items that can be included in the Control panel; specific items appear when specific tools are used. If, for some reason, you decide you want to hide any of these items, just click them in the list to remove the item's checkmark. If you decide to show the item again, open this menu and click the item name.

To tear off the Control panel and float it anywhere on the screen: Press on the dotted finger grip located on the far-left side of the Control panel (shown below), then drag the panel away from its current position to anywhere on the screen.

✓ Dock To Top
  Dock To Bottom

✓ Align
✓ Anchor Points
✓ Artboard
✓ Brush
✓ Character
✓ Clipping Mask
✓ Document
✓ Envelope Distort
✓ Fill and Stroke
✓ FlashText
✓ Focus Mode
✓ Graphic Style
✓ Image
✓ Live Paint Group
✓ Merge Live Paint
✓ Object Type
✓ Paragraph
✓ Perspective
✓ Recolor Artwork
✓ Select Same
✓ Symbols
✓ Tracing
✓ Transform
✓ Transparency
✓ Width Profile

To put the Control panel back, drag it to the top of the screen until a blue bar appears, then release. The panel snaps to the blue bar position.

When the blue bar appears, the panel will snap to that position.

The Tools panel

The **Tools panel**, usually located on the left side of the document window, contains all the tools you'll need. Or, to be more precise, the Tools panel contains gobs more tools than you'll ever need for any project. Or lifetime.

The most useful and most commonly used tools are explained in upcoming exercises, but some tools are not within the scope of this book, such as Graph tools, Perspective Drawing tools, and 3D tools.

How to select hidden tools

A tiny black triangle in the lower-right corner of a tool icon indicates there are even *more* tools that are grouped with this icon, but they are **hidden.** To show the hidden tools, **press** *(don't click)* on the tool icon, slide the pointer over one of the hidden tools (still pressing), then let go of the mouse or trackpad button.

You can also cycle through the hidden tools: hold down the Option key (PC: Alt key) as you click a tool icon. Each click reveals and selects the next hidden tool.

TASK 3   Create a floating panel of the tools in a group

1   *Press* on a tool icon, then slide the pointer (while still pressing) to the right edge of the hidden tools flyout menu.

2   When the right edge of the hidden tools menu (the tearoff strip, as shown below) turns dark, let go. A floating Tools panel replaces the flyout panel.

3   Drag the title bar of the floating panel to move it.

4   To close the floating panel, just click the red button.

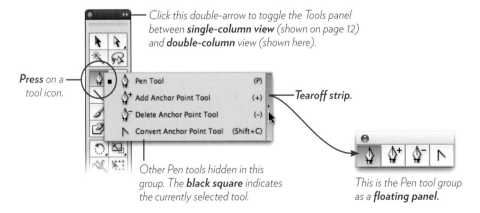

Click this double-arrow to toggle the *Tools* panel between **single-column view** (shown on page 12) and **double-column** view (shown here).

Press on a tool icon.

Pen Tool (P)

Add Anchor Point Tool (+)

Delete Anchor Point Tool (-)

Convert Anchor Point Tool (Shift+C)

Tearoff strip.

Other Pen tools hidden in this group. The **black square** indicates the currently selected tool.

This is the Pen tool group as a **floating panel**.

The Fill and Stroke color attributes

When you start creating objects, you'll be using the **Fill and Stroke options** constantly to put color inside objects (the fill) or borders around the objects (the stroke), so you want to become familiar with the Fill and Stroke icons in the Tools panel. These icons overlap each other; the one on top is the *active* attribute that shows the color of the *selected* object, and it is also the attribute that will get *applied* when you choose a new color, as explained below.

To choose a new color for selected objects (or objects you are about to create), double-click the Fill color icon *or* the Stroke color icon to make it active *and* open the Color Picker. Choose a color; click OK. The new color appears in the icon. See Chapter 11 for details on color.

To switch the Fill and Stroke colors, click the tiny double-headed arrow in the upper-right corner of the icons. *Or* tap the X key.

To reset Fill and Stroke colors to factory default settings (white fill, black stroke), click the teeny icon called out below. *Or* tap the D key.

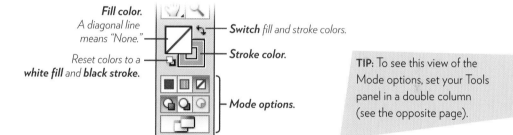

Fill color.
A diagonal line means "None."

Reset colors to a white fill and **black stroke.**

Switch fill and stroke colors.

Stroke color.

Mode options.

TIP: To see this view of the Mode options, set your Tools panel in a double column (see the opposite page).

The Mode options

The bottom section of the Tools panel provides several **mode options.** The **Color mode options** (buttons in the top row), explained in Chapter 11, are to apply color and gradients to artwork. The **Drawing mode options** (the middle row) switch between *Normal* mode, *Draw Behind,* or *Draw Inside,* as explained in Chapter 6. But you can experiment with the **Screen mode options** right now:

TASK 4   Change the screen mode options

1   Single-click the bottom button in the Tools panel. In the pop-up menu that appears, choose one of the modes to view your project in full screen, with or without menu bars, or back to a normal view.

2   To quickly toggle between screen modes, tap the F key. Try it!

Managing your workspace panels

Illustrator provides lots of panels: the Tools panel, the Control panel, and myriad panels in a vertical dock on the right side of the window. All available panels are listed in the Window menu.

The specific panels that appear in the vertical dock are determined by the workspace layout you choose from the Workspace Switcher in the Control panel (see pages 14 and 15). You can add additional panels to any workspace at any time. Because you will be opening, closing panels, and docking panels constantly, take a few minutes to practice working with them.

TASK 5 Learn to control the panels

Knowing how to manage panels makes your workflow more efficient.

1 **Add another panel to your workspace:** Go to the Window menu and choose the panel you want. It appears as a floating panel (below, left) or it pops out from the dock on the side (below, right).

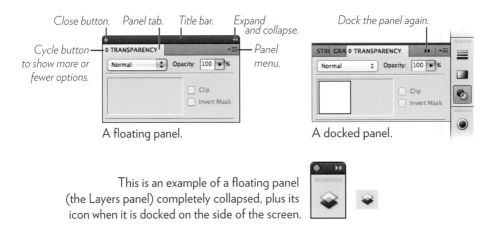

Close button.   Panel tab.   Title bar.   Expand and collapse.   Dock the panel again.

Cycle button to show more or fewer options.

Panel menu.

A floating panel.   A docked panel.

This is an example of a floating panel (the Layers panel) completely collapsed, plus its icon when it is docked on the side of the screen.

2 **To close a floating panel,** click the round button on the upper-left corner of the panel, shown above-left.
To close a docked panel, click the right-pointing double-arrow symbol, shown above-right (I call that the *re-dock button*).
To reopen a closed panel, choose it from the Window menu again, *or* single-click an icon in the panel dock.

3 **To collapse or expand a floating panel,** double-click its title bar.

4 **To float a panel that is docked,** drag the panel icon out of the vertical dock, then drop it anywhere in the window. Double-click its title bar to expand it.

5 **To expand a panel,** double-click its title bar.

   To further expand a panel and show even more options, click the tiny *cycle button* on the tab, shown opposite. Each click expands the panel another level, *if* the panel includes multiple levels.

   To instantly expand a panel to its maximum, double-click the dark gray area to the right of the name tab.

6 Create **groups** of like-minded panels so you can have them easily accessible for projects:

   To group a panel to another panel, drag a title bar on top of another panel icon, between docked icons, or into the name tab. Drag the panel until a blue bar appears where you want to drop the panel, then let go.

   To ungroup a panel from a group and float it, drag its name tab out of the group, then drop it somewhere else in the window.

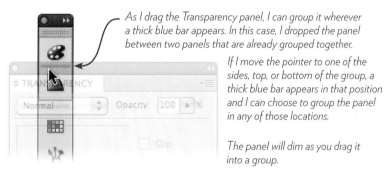

As I drag the Transparency panel, I can group it wherever a thick blue bar appears. In this case, I dropped the panel between two panels that are already grouped together.

If I move the pointer to one of the sides, top, or bottom of the group, a thick blue bar appears in that position and I can choose to group the panel in any of those locations.

The panel will dim as you drag it into a group.

Double-click the blank gray tab area to collapse the panel group.

The collapsed panel group.

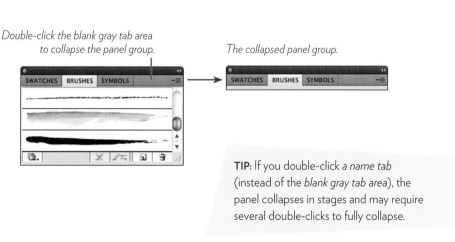

TIP: If you double-click *a name tab* (instead of the *blank gray tab area*), the panel collapses in stages and may require several double-clicks to fully collapse.

Working with artboards

Artboards are similar to pages in other applications, such as InDesign. You can create as many artboards as you need, up to 100, depending on their sizes. Each artboard can be a different size; for instance, you might have a logo design project that includes separate artboards for the logo, the letterhead design, and the business card design, all in one document (as shown below). Or you might want seven variations of the same project open in one file; put each one on a separate artboard.

Each artboard prints as an individual page. They are numbered in the Artboard panel, and you can change their order number (see page 22).

Keep in mind that artboards are *not* like pages in that every artboard you create in one Illustrator document appears on the screen at the same time. If you have lots of large artboards in one document, you'll be scrolling a lot.

The area outside the artboards is the **canvas.** *Elements placed on the canvas don't print, nor do they appear when you export the art.*

The selected (active) artboard has a dotted border with handles. Drag any handle to resize that artboard. When the Artboard tool is chosen, artboards display a name label in the upper-left corner, and the canvas area turns dark gray.

Because the artboard is the basic surface on which you will be creating your work, it's a good idea to spend several minutes experimenting with the many mini-tasks on these pages so you feel comfortable working with them.

TASK 6   Use the Artboard tool

Select the Artboard tool in the Tools panel to resize, reposition, or rename artboards.

 The Artboard tool.

- **To resize an artboard:** With the Artboard tool, click the artboard you want to resize to make it active. In the Control panel, type the new dimensions you want to use.

Editable measurements appear in the Control panel when the Artboard tool is selected.

- **To visually resize an artboard** to fit more snugly around existing art, select the Artboard tool, click an artboard to make it active, then drag its handles.
- **To rename an artboard,** double-click the Artboard tool. In the "Artboard Options" dialog box that appears, rename the artboard, change its size, and modify a few other options if you want.
- **To reposition an artboard,** with the Artboard tool, drag the artboard to another position on the canvas.

TASK 7   Create more artboards

As you saw in Tasks 1 and 2, the "New Document" dialog box lets you specify the number of artboards. **To create one or more additional artboards at any time,** experiment with the following:

- Choose the Artboard tool from the Tools panel, then drag on the canvas to create the size and shape artboard you want.
- With the Artboard tool, Option-drag (PC: Alt-drag) an existing artboard on the canvas to create a copy.
- Double-click the Artboard tool to open the "Artboard Options" dialog box. Select an artboard from the "Preset" pop-up menu.

TASK 8   Use the Artboards panel

The Artboards panel shows a list of all artboards in the document.
Try each of these tasks:

- **To rearrange the artboards numerically** (although this won't change
  their positions on the canvas), drag items in the list up or down.
- **To delete an artboard**, select an artboard name in the list, then click
  the Trash icon in the lower-right corner.
- **To create a new artboard**, click the "New Artboard" icon at the bottom
  of the panel.
- **To open the "Artboard Options" dialog box for a specific artboard,**
  click the document icon to the right of the artboard name.
- **To access the commands and options** shown in the menu below,
  click the Artboard panel menu (in the panel's top-right corner).

New Artboard.

Another way to create a
new artboard.

You can also drag an existing
artboard and drop it on
the New Artboard *icon*
to create a duplicate.

TASK 9   Select the artboard you want

You need to select the artboard to alter it or work on it. Try each of these
methods for selecting the board.

- In the document window, scroll to the artboard you want.
- Open the Artboards panel, then single-click the name you want to use.
- To fill the document window with a specific artboard, double-click its
  name in the Artboards panel list.
- Open the Navigator panel (Window > Navigator) and single-click an
  artboard in that panel.
- Click the artboard number in the status bar (in the lower-left corner of
  the document window). From the pop-up menu (shown below), select
  the artboard you want.

TASK 10   Hide or show artboards

You can hide artboards and still work as usual—you just won't see the gray canvas. This doesn't hide any art—all the art from all the artboards will appear to be on a seamless white background. Choose View > Hide Artboards; to restore them, choose View > Show Artboards.

TASK 11   Save an artboard as a separate file

During a project, you may want to save one or more artboards as a separate file. That's easy to do.

1   Choose File > Save As… (or choose File > Save a Copy…).

2   In the "Save As" dialog box, give the file a new name and choose where to save it. From the Format pop-up menu, choose "Adobe Illustrator (ai)." Click ok.

3   In the "Illustrator Options" dialog box that appears (below), check the box to "Save each artboard to a separate file."

4   Choose "All," or choose "Range" to specify certain artboards to save. Use a hyphen or commas to specify the range; e.g., 1-3 or 1,4,5,7.

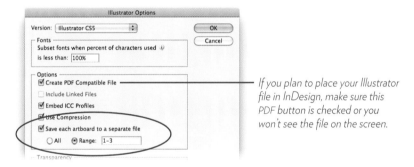

If you plan to place your Illustrator file in InDesign, make sure this PDF button is checked or you won't see the file on the screen.

Artboard rulers vs Global rulers

To show rulers in the document window, choose View > Rulers > Show Rulers. There are two kinds of rulers in Illustrator: artboard and global.

A **global ruler** stretches across all artboards. Its origin point is the top-left corner of the first artboard on the left. To change the global ruler origin point, drag crosshairs from the top-left corner of the rulers to a point where you want the ruler origin point to start.

To change to **artboard rulers,** choose View > Rulers > Change to Artboard Rulers. The origin point of an artboard ruler is the top-left corner *of the currently active artboard.* Click anywhere in an artboard to reset the artboard ruler origin point to that artboard.

Guides to guide you

Guides are indispensable during Nepal treks, past-life regressions, and Illustrator projects. In Illustrator, you can create horizontal or vertical non-printing guides with which to align objects. You can also turn custom art into non-printing, snapable guides (very handy when horizontal and vertical guides just don't cut it). And there are Smart Guides that appear only when you need them.

TASK 12   Create guides

1   To create guides, first show the rulers (see the previous page).

2   Position the pointer on one of the rulers (the vertical ruler on the left side of the document or the horizontal ruler across the top of the window), then press-and-drag into the artboard area.

A guide line drags out of the ruler and into the document. Release the mouse button when the guide is positioned where you want it.

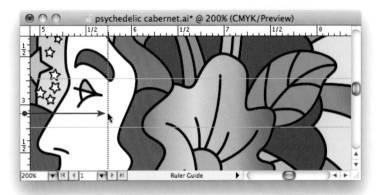

3   **To move a guide,** get the black Selection tool (the black arrow), then press-and-drag the guide.

4   **To delete a guide,** select it with the black Selection tool, then hit the Delete key (PC: Backspace key).

5   **To lock the guides** so you don't accidentally move them, use the View > Guides menu and choose "Lock Guides" (also use that menu to **unlock** the guides).

Snap to guides

You can tell objects to *snap* to guidelines when they get close, which is really handy. Choose View > Snap to Point (if there is a checkmark next to that command, it is on). This setting makes objects snap to *both* points and guides.

If this snapping action makes it hard to place an object where you want it, choose the setting again to turn it off.

Create custom guides

Horizontal and vertical guides are usually all you need, but occasionally custom guides, such as angles or curves, come in handy in certain drawing projects such as maps or solar sytems.

1   **To create custom guides**, draw lines with a drawing tool, such as the Line tool (explained in Chapter 4) or the Pen tool (explained in Chapter 5).

2   With the black Selection tool, select the lines.

3   Choose View > Guides > Make. The artwork is converted to guides that are non-printing, and you can snap to them as any other guide.

Guides of all sorts are useful in projects such as maps.

Be smart, use Smart Guides

When Smart Guides are turned on, temporary green guidelines appear as you move objects, telling you when they are aligned with something else. Smart Guides can point out center alignments, side alignments, and more.

TASK 13   Use Smart Guides to align multiple objects

1   Create a new document of any size, or use one that's already open.

2   Select the Rectangle tool in the Tools panel.

3   Draw three rectangles, as shown below: Press-and-drag diagonally to create the rectangular shapes; let go when done with each shape.

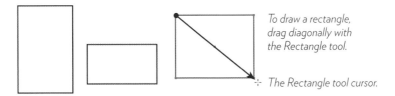

To draw a rectangle, drag diagonally with the Rectangle tool.

The Rectangle tool cursor.

4   Activate Smart Guides, if they're not already on: Choose View > Smart Guides. (Learn the keyboard shortcut because you'll be wanting to turn them on and off regularly as you work.)

5   Align the top edges of two rectangles: Drag one of the rectangles until a green Smart Guide appears, indicating the top edge is aligned with another rectangle's top edge (shown below).

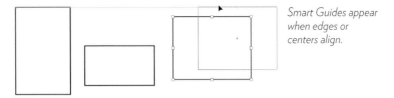

Smart Guides appear when edges or centers align.

To change the color of Smart Guides, choose Illustrator > Preferences > Smart Guides (PC: Edit > Preferences > Smart Guides). From the "Color" pop-up menu, choose a color.

While you're in that dialog box, also consider deselecting two of the other options that can create a lot of visual clutter, "Anchor/Path Labels" and "Measurement Labels." These are the options that create those **little green words** all over the place.

TIP: If the Smart Guides aren't working even when they are turned on in the menu, you probably have "Snap To Grid" or "Pixel Preview" turned on (View menu). Turn those off to make Smart Guides work.

3 Learn to be Selective

It may seem premature to talk about *paths* and *segments* and *shapes* and *points* and how to *select* individual parts of each, but what you learn in this short chapter applies to everything you will ever do in Illustrator. You will select paths and shapes to assign color and fill attributes, as well as to modify objects in various ways to create your amazing art. All subsequent chapters in this book build upon what you learn about vector artwork here.

We advise you to read through this chapter so you know what the possibilities are and so you know where you can find the information when you need it. Trying to select exactly the paths you need when you've got a complex illustration can be hugely frustrating if you don't know the precise techniques.

Selecting objects

At least half of what you do in Illustrator is **select** the vector objects you've created so you can modify them in some way. In the next chapter, we'll start drawing some objects, but first it's really important to understand the parts of a vector path and how to select its different parts.

Open and closed paths

Every vector object, simple or complex, is composed of **paths** which are defined in the file mathematically. Every path is either a **closed path** or an **open path.** You can usually tell the difference by looking at them, as shown below. Selection techniques are the same for both kinds of objects.

A **closed path** has **no end point.** It could hold water (theoretically).

An **open path** has **two end points.** It couldn't hold water at all.

The anatomy of a path

All paths are made of path **segments,** which can be straight or curved, and **anchor points.** Anchor points can be *corner points* (to create sudden changes in the path direction), *smooth points* (to create smooth changes in the path direction), or *cusp points* (to combine a corner point and smooth point).

An unselected path is actually invisible; what you see is the **stroke** that has been applied to the path. The path below has a 5-point gold stroke applied to it.

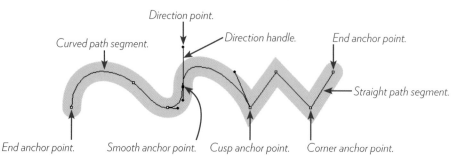

Direction point.

Curved path segment.

Direction handle.

End anchor point.

Straight path segment.

End anchor point.   *Smooth anchor point.*   *Cusp anchor point.*   *Corner anchor point.*

- **Smooth points,** when selected, have **direction handles** on *both* sides of the point. Drag handles to adjust the adjacent curved segments.

- **Cusp points** connect a curved segment and a straight segment and have **one direction handle** coming out on the curved side. Drag the handle to adjust the curved segment only.

- **Corner points** connect path segments that change direction; they have no direction handles.

- Drag anchor points to reposition them.
- Drag a path segment to alter adjacent segments.
- *Selected* anchor points are black, *unselected* anchor points are white.

Using the Selection tools

When a path is *not* selected, all you see is its stroke (and its fill, if it has one). **To see the actual path** (shown below, right), select it with one of the selection tools—the black Selection tool or the white Direct Selection tool.

 The **black Selection tool** (the black arrow) selects *entire paths.* Use this tool when you want to select an entire path or shape as an object.

When the **Selection tool** hovers *exactly* on a **path**, a tiny black square appears next to the pointer (above, left). Click to select the entire path (above, right).

To select an object without hovering to search for a path location, use the Selection tool to **drag a marquee** around a section of the object (above, left). Release the mouse to select the underlying path (above, right).

 The **white Direct Selection tool** (the white arrow) selects *path segments* or individual *anchor points.*

When the **Direct Selection tool** hovers exactly on a **path**, a small black square appears next to the pointer (left). Click to select that specific path segment (right).

When the **Direct Selection tool** hovers exactly on an **anchor point**, a small white square appears next to the pointer, and the anchor point appears under the tip of the pointer (above, left). Click to select that specific anchor point (above, right).

Marquee with the **Direct Selection tool** around a section of a path (left). Release to select path segments and anchors that are within the marqeed area (right).

TIP: You can select an entire path with the white Direct Selection tool: Hold down the Option key [PC: Alt key] and click the path.

Select an entire shape

To select an entire shape, do one of the following:

- With *either* of the Selection arrows (black or white), marquee around the entire shape to select all anchor points and path segments.

- With the *black* Selection tool, click any part of the shape's path.

- With the *white* Direct Selection tool, Option-click (PC: Alt-click) any part of the shape's path.

- With either of the Selection tools, click the shape's *fill color.*
  (If this doesn't work, it's because the option called "Object Selection by Path Only" is checked in Illustrator's Preferences > Selection & Anchor Display. When this preference is selected, the only way to select an object is to click or marquee its path—not its fill color.)

Select part of a group

Illustrations are usually made up of a huge number of shapes. You will often **group** shapes (page 33) so they are easier to select, modify, or move. When you click on a group with the *black* Selection tool, the entire group is selected, as shown below-left.

But then you discover that you need to select a specific path or shape within a group—use the trusty *white* Direct Selection tool. **To select one path segment**, use the *white* Direct Selection tool and click the path of one of the grouped shapes (below, center). **To select the entire path** of one of the grouped shapes, Option-click (PC: Alt-click) the path, as shown below-right.

Grouped objects.   *Select a path segment.*   *Select an entire path.*

What did you just select?

Just to be clear, let's review what exactly you've selected when you use these different selection techniques.

The black Selection tool

To select all of a shape's paths and anchor points, use the *black* Selection tool and click a shape's path (below, left). If multiple shapes have been *grouped* (below, right), the Selection tool selects everything in the group.

Objects and groups selected with the black Selection tool display a bounding box around the objects.

To temporarily hide the bounding box, press the Command key (PC: Control key).

The white Direct Selection tool

To select a specific object, use the *white* Direct Selection tool and click a shape's path, even if it's part of a group (left).

With the path selected, you can change the object's fill or stroke attributes. However, if you try to move the object, it will distort because this is really only a *partial* selection—a single segment or anchor point is selected, *not* the entire shape.

To make a complete selection of an object, in which all path segments and anchors are selected, use the white Direct Selection tool, press the Option key (PC: Alt key), and click the path (left). With the Option/Alt key held down, a small plus symbol appears next to the Direct Selection tool pointer. This indicates that all path segments and anchors will be selected *in addition* to the path segment or anchor you click.

The Outline mode for easier selecting

You'll typically work on your art in **Preview mode,** in color, just as it will appear when printed, exported, or saved for a web page, mobile device, or InDesign layout. But it's often easier to select paths if you view artwork in **Outline mode.**

To switch the view to **Outline mode,** choose View > Outline. The outline view displays the paths that make up the illustration, without showing any fills or strokes. This view can be helpful when you need to select paths that are covered by other shapes and hidden in Preview mode, especially in highly complex art. You can work in Outline mode, which might make it easier to align anchor points or paths when necessary.

To return to Preview mode, choose View > Preview.

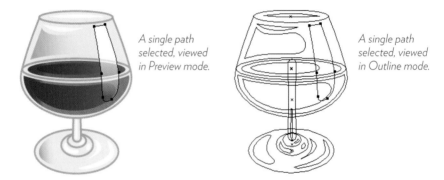

A single path selected, viewed in Preview mode.

A single path selected, viewed in Outline mode.

Select similar objects

To easily select *similar* objects in complex artwork, first *select* an object, then choose Select > Same > Fill (or choose one of the other attribute options in the submenu). Illustrator automatically finds and selects all objects that have the same fill attributes as the *selected* object.

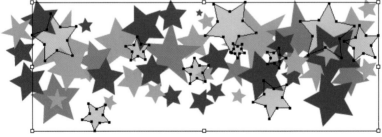

I selected one gold star, then chose Select > Same > Fill to find others of the same color.

Create groups

When artwork gets complex with lots of paths, it's best to *group* related paths together so they're easier to select.

To create a group: With the black Selection tool, select all the paths you want to include in the group (Shift-click multiple paths or marquee around them). Choose Object > Group.

To release a group: Select the group (click anywhere on it with the Selection tool), then choose Object > Ungroup.

To select the paths you want to group, marquee them (above), or Shift-select the paths.

With the paths selected and grouped, it's easy to select the group and move it.

The selected group, repositioned.

The Group Selection tool

The Group Selection tool makes it easy to select groups within other groups. In the example below, the veins of the leaf are a group, and that group is grouped with the leaf shape, making it easier to select the entire leaf with a single click of the Selection tool.

TASK 1 Select a group within a group

1 Choose the Group Selection tool (it's hidden under the white Direct Selection tool in the Tools panel).

2 Click one of the paths in a group; that path is selected (below, left).

3 Click the *same* place a second time. The parent *group* is selected (below, center). Click the *same* place a third time to add the leaf shape that's grouped with the leaf veins (below, right).

First click. *Second click.* *Third click.*

The Select menu

Spend some time to become familiar with the Select menu and its selection options, so when you get to a point where you need to select a particular item, you'll know what your options are.

- **All** selects everything on *all* artboards.
- **All on Active Artboard** selects everything on *just* the active artboard (the one that is currently selected).
- **Deselect** does just that, deselects anything selected.
- **Reselect** applies the same selection options (options found in the "Same" submenu, shown below) of a previous selection to the next selection you make.

  For example, suppose you use the "Same" command (see below) to select all objects with a certain fill color, such as red. If, later, you again want to select all objects filled with red, you can choose Select > Reselect and all objects with a red fill are selected.
- **Inverse** *deselects* all selections and *selects* everything *else* (on all artboards). This is handy, for instance, when you have an object that you *do not* want to apply a transformation to: Select that object, and then choose Inverse to deselect it and select everything else.
- **Next Object Above** selects the next object in the stacking order *above* the selected object. This is really tricky because in a complex piece of art, it is almost impossible to tell what the stacking order is.
- **Next Object Below** selects the next object in the stacking order below the selected object. See the note, above.
- **Same** selects objects that have the same attributes as an object you've selected. Choose "Same," then select one of the attributes listed in the flyout menu (shown below). This applies to all artboards.
- **Object** provides a submenu of different kinds of objects you can choose to select (Brush Strokes, Text Objects, etc.).

Save a selection to use again

In a complex illustration, it can be tedious selecting a number of individual paths (or even finding one particular path) that you want to change. If you suspect that you might want to select the same path (or paths) at some time in the future, you can add the selection to the Select menu.

TASK 2   Save a selection

1   Select one or more paths or objects.

2   Choose Select > Save Selection….

3   In the "Save Selection" dialog box that opens, name the selection, then click OK.

The name of the saved selection now appears at the bottom of the Select menu. The next time you want to select that particular path (or paths), go to the Select menu, and click the name of your saved selection at the bottom of the menu.

Saved selections.

TIP: **To remove a saved option from the Select menu,** go to the Select menu and choose, "Edit Selection…." Click the name of the selection you want to remove, click "Delete," then click OK.

After saving this selection of stars, I can select the same stars at any time by selecting the "stars" item at the bottom of the Select menu.

Change the color of selection edges

Each layer in the Layers panel (see Chapter 9 for details on Layers) is automatically assigned a color to highlight selection edges and anchor points, but sometimes the assigned color doesn't show up against the stroke or fill color of your artwork. For example, if you're working with a thick black stroke and the selection edges color is black, it's hard to see paths and anchor points; in that case, you might want to change the colors (or switch to Outline preview mode; see page 32).

TASK 3 Change the color used to show selection edges

1   In the Layers panel, double-click the layer that contains the art you're working with.

2   In the "Layers Options" dialog box that opens, choose a contrasting color from the "Color" pop-up menu. Click OK.

This stroke is selected, but its selection edges are black so I can't see the path.

Once I changed the selection edges to red, I could see the path within the stroke.

Hide or show selection edges

When an object is selected, its edges and anchor points are highlighted in a color, as shown above-right. But sometimes the highlighted edges can get in the way, visually speaking, especially when you're experimenting with different fills or stroke colors to apply to the selection. **To see the artwork without distractions,** you can hide the selection edges: Go to the View menu and choose "Hide Edges." Learn the keyboard shortcut to hide or show the edges because it will come in handy: Command H (PC: Control H).

Bring to Front and Send to Back

Last, but certainly not least, you will discover that you regularly need to select an object and send it behind another object or bring it in front, so get to know the Arrange options in the Object menu. "Bring Forward" or "Send Backward" move the selected object in front of or behind just one item in the stack; to bring the object all the way to the front or send it all the way to the back, choose "Bring to Front" or "Send to Back."

Section 2
Drawing Vector Art

A Midsummer Night's Dream

Vector art drawing gives you the power to easily develop artwork with accuracy, and to create effects that would otherwise be very difficult. It provides flexibility that enables you to experiment, make changes, and create multiple versions of a project. And it provides the convenience of creating one file that can be used with various media types, large or small.

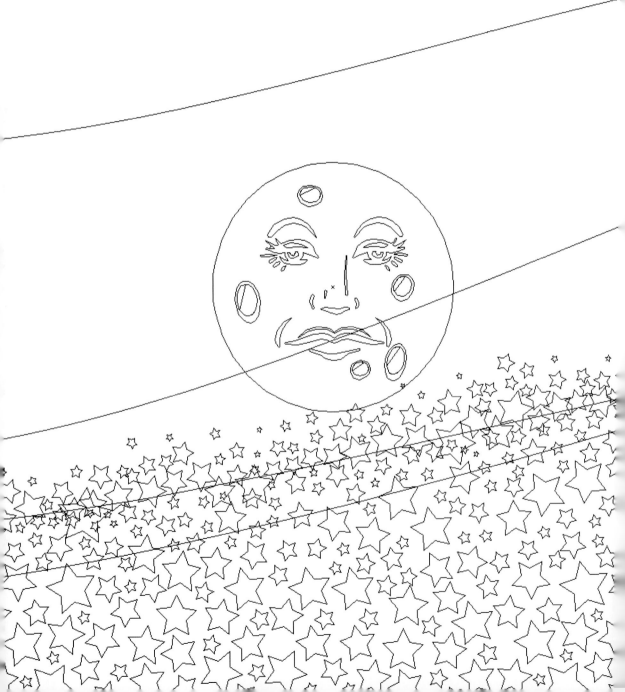

4 Drawing with Shape and Line Tools

Illustrator provides tools for easily creating lines and shapes. Drawing with shapes (rectangles, ellipses, stars, etc.) can be a surprisingly creative and satisfying solution, especially if you don't think you can draw. It can be even more effective than drawing with felt-tip pens in a style that won somebody [that would be John] a potted plant in a fifth-grade poster contest.

If you feel that you're drawing-challenged, follow the tasks in this chapter and then play with the tools—you'll discover that you're able to create all sorts of amazingly creative and useful images.

TIP: Some drawing techniques are *so* much easier if you use a pressure-sensitive tablet, such as a Wacom tablet. When drawing paths with the Pen tool, we prefer a mouse, but for the tools that require brush-like strokes, a tablet makes a gigantic difference in the results.

Drawing with shape tools

Let's start by using some of the shape tools from the Tools panel. As you do the tasks in this chapter, you'll be introduced to lots of panels and settings that you'll use in every project.

These exercises start your vector drawing career. The simple steps included here are used to some degree in every vector drawing.

TASK 1 Draw a rectangle

1 Select the Rectangle tool from the Tools panel.

2 Drag diagonally in any direction.

Release the mouse after you create a horizontal rectangle.

And there you go—a rectangle with a default white fill and a 1-point black stroke. Your rectangle might have a different color fill and stroke.

TASK 2 Apply fill and stroke attributes to the rectangle

1 With the black Selection tool, single-click the rectangle to select it.

2 Click the *Fill Color* pop-up menu in the Control panel (shown below), then choose a color from the swatches panel that opens.

3 While the rectangle is still selected, click the *Stroke Color* pop-up menu in the Control panel, then choose a color from the swatches panel that opens.

4 From the "Stroke" weight pop-up menu, choose 6 pt.
Or tap the Up/Down arrows to the left of the stroke weight.
Or type 6 in the value field (you don't have to type the "pt."

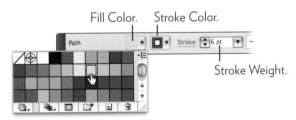

Fill Color.   Stroke Color.

Stroke Weight.

The rectangle with new fill and stroke attributes.

TASK 3   Draw a perfect square

1   With the Rectangle tool, hold down the Shift key as you drag a shape.

2   Add the Option key (PC: Alt key) as you drag to change the origin point from a corner to the center of the square.

TIP: When the tip of the black Selection tool is near a corner of a selected object, the cursor turns into a **curved double arrow,** as shown to the left. Press-and-drag with that cursor to **rotate** the object.

TASK 4   Draw a perfect circle

1   Select the Ellipse tool (it's hidden under the Rectangle tool).

2   Drag diagonally in any direction.

To constrain the ellipse to a perfect circle, hold down the Shift key as you drag.

To make the center of the circle the origin point as you drag, hold down the Option key (PC: Alt key) as well.

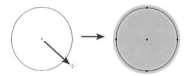

TASK 5   Draw a rounded rectangle

1   Select the Rounded Rectangle tool (it's under the Rectangle tool).

2   Drag diagonally to create a rectangle.

To constrain the shape to a rounded square, hold down the Shift key as you drag. **To make the center of the shape the origin point** of the drag, hold down the Option key (PC: Alt key).

3   **To change the radius of the corners as you drag,** tap the up or down arrows on the keyboard before you let go of the mouse/trackpad.

Two rounded rectangles, each with a different corner radius.

TIP: If you change the fill and stroke colors *before* you create a shape (make sure nothing is selected), all new shapes will be drawn with those chosen attributes.

TASK 6 Draw star shapes

1 Select the Star tool (it's under the Rectangle tool in the Tools panel).

2 Drag diagonally in any direction.

 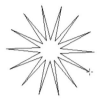

To rotate the star shape as you draw, drag the Star tool in an arc. Hold down the Shift key to prevent any rotation.

Above, left: **To increase the radius** *of the innermost points, hold down the Command key (PC: Control key) as you drag* **inward.**

Above, right: **To decrease the radius** *of the innermost points, hold down the Command (PC: Control key) as you drag* **outward.**

To add or remove points, tap the up or down arrow keys as you drag.

Use the white Direct Selection tool to drag any anchor point to reshape that point.

The Star tool is a one-stop star-shopping experience.

TIP for drawing shapes

Using visual judgment to draw shapes works most of the time, but if you need to create a shape with precise numerical control, it's good to know that each of the shape drawing tools provides a dialog box of numerical options.

Select a shape tool from the Tools panel, then single-click in your document window. A dialog box opens with numerical fields. Enter the values you want, then click OK.

The new shape appears in your document.

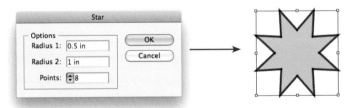

TASK 7 Modify shapes

Once you've created a shape, you can modify it whenever and however you want. When creating artwork, it's often best to start with basic shapes, then make changes to the shapes.

1 Draw a perfect circle (see Task 4 on page 41), then apply any fill and stroke color you want (Task 2, page 40). Set the stroke size thick enough that you can easily see the path within the stroke.

With the white Direct Selection tool, select the circle's path (as explained in Chapter 3). Then practice the manipulations shown below.

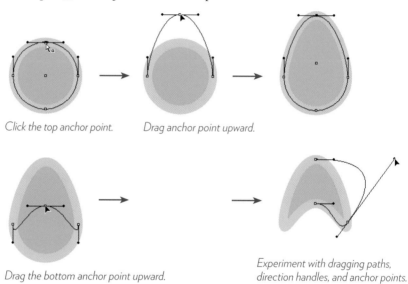

Click the top anchor point.   Drag anchor point upward.

Drag the bottom anchor point upward.

Experiment with dragging paths, direction handles, and anchor points.

2 Draw a rectangle (see Task 1, page 40). With the white Direct Selection tool, modify the shape as shown below.

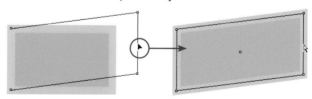

Select a **path,** then drag to another position.

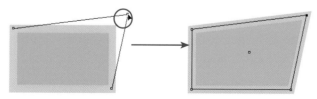

Select an **anchor point,** then drag to another position.

Drawing with line tools

A collection of line tools are grouped together in the Tools panel, hidden under the Line Segment tool. Even though you won't use all of these tools very often, you'll find some of them to be powerful and useful.

Press (don't click) on the Line Segment tool to see and select the other line tools.

The Line Segment tool

The Line Segment tool draws a straight line. You can drag to create lines, as instructed below, or use the "Line Segment Tool Options" dialog box.

TASK 8   Draw straight lines

a. Use the "Line Segment Tool Options" dialog box to create straight lines:

1   Choose the Line Segment tool in the Tools panel, then single-click in a document to open the "Line Segment Tool Options" dialog box.

2   Enter a line length and choose an angle, then click OK. The specified line appears in your document.

3   While the line segment is selected (you can see the end points), practice giving it different stroke colors and widths.

This is a line segment.

b. Or simply drag to quickly create straight lines:

4   With the Line Segment tool, position the pointer where you want the line to begin, then press-and-drag to the point where you want the line to end.

   Shift-drag to constrain the drawing of the line segment to a horizontal, 45° diagonal, or vertical line.

5   Change the stroke color or size: Make sure the line is still selected, then use the Control panel stroke controls (see Task 2, page 40).

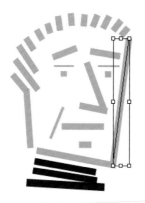

The Line Segment tool isn't usually used to create an illustration, but it can be, as shown by this drawing of a creative person (black turtleneck = creative type).

ART TIP: Illustration doesn't have to be complex. Simplicity can be just as interesting as photo-realism. OK, maybe not here, but sometimes.

TASK 9   Add arrowheads to a straight line segment

You can turn straight lines created with the Line Segment tool into directional arrows.

1 Draw a straight line (see Task 8 on the opposite page).

2 Click the word "Stroke" in the Control panel to open the Stroke panel.

3 In the Stroke flyout panel (below), choose styles from the "Arrowheads" pop-up menus. Choose a style for both the start and end of the path.

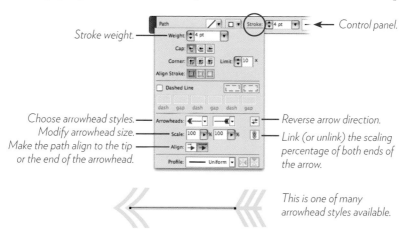

Stroke weight.

Control panel.

Choose arrowhead styles.
Modify arrowhead size.
Make the path align to the tip or the end of the arrowhead.

Reverse arrow direction.

Link (or unlink) the scaling percentage of both ends of the arrow.

This is one of many arrowhead styles available.

4 To remove an arrowhead from a path: Select an arrow in your document, click "Stroke" in the Control panel, then choose "None" from the "Arrowheads" pop-up menus in the Stroke panel (above).

The Spiral tool

The Spiral tool makes drawing spirals easy, and a little confusing. You'll need some practice to be able to predict the results of using this tool, but perhaps its organic unpredictability is part of the magic and ancient symbolism of the spiral shape.

TASK 10   Draw spirals

1   Choose the Spiral tool (see page 44).

2   Drag in the document to create a spiral; move the tool around to tilt the spiral. Keep holding the tool down while you do this:

>   **To add rings to a spiral**, tap the UpArrow.
>
>   **To remove rings from a spiral**, tap the DownArrow.
>
>   **To tighten the spiral**, hold down the Command key
>   (PC: Control key) and drag in toward the center of the spiral.
>
>   **To loosen the spiral**, hold down the Command key
>   (PC: Control key) and drag outward, away from the center.

You'll see the changes happen live in outline view mode. Use the Stroke settings in the Control panel to color and stroke the path.

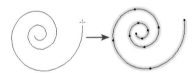

When you drag, the spiral is shown in outline mode (above, left). When you release, the preview version is visible (above, right).

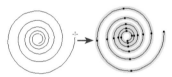

Without letting go of the cursor, tap the up or down arrows to add or remove spirals.

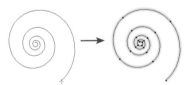

To loosen the spirals, hold down the Command key (PC: Control key) and drag outward, away from the center.

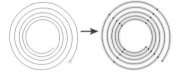

To tighten the spirals, hold down the Command key (PC: Control key) and drag inward, toward the center.

TASK 11 Control the spiral shapes

The Spiral tool draws with the settings in the "Spiral" dialog box, so it's a good idea to play with those settings and see if you can control the results.

1 With the Spiral tool, click on the page to open the "Spiral" dialog box.

2 Since there's no preview pane to show what kind of spiral your settings will create, start with the settings shown below.

3 Click OK. The spiral immediately appears in your document. **To change the color or size of the spiral stroke,** use the Stroke options in the Control bar.

Distance from the center to the outermost point. ——
The tightness of the spiral. ——
The number of segments determines how many spirals are present; it takes four segments to make one wind. ——

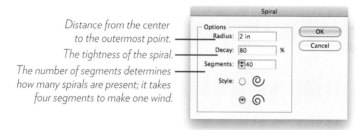

TASK 12 Modify a spiral with the Width tool

This is a quick introduction to the Width tool (more in Chapter 7), a special tool that makes part of a path thinner or thicker wherever you choose.

1 Use the black Selection tool to select one of the spirals you created.

2 Select the Width tool from the Tools panel, then hover the tool over the spiral path. When the tool is over a path, the end point becomes a white square and the cursor gets a little plus mark (below, left).

3 Press on the white square and drag the Width tool handles *away* from the path to make the stroke at that location thicker (below, right). The stroke automatically tapers gradually to its original width.

You can actually press anywhere in the path and widen or narrow it at that point.

TIP: When drawing with any of the Shape or Line tools, you can reposition the object you're drawing—on the fly: As you drag, hold down the Spacebar (continue to press the mouse), then move the object to any position. When you release the Spacebar (still pressing the mouse), you can continue modifying the shape.

The Arc tool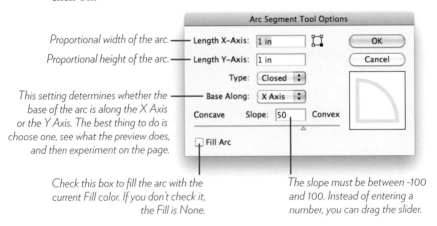

The Arc tool draws arcs of all sorts. You can draw an arc as an open path or as a closed path (open and closed paths are explained on page 28).

TASK 13   Draw convex and concave arcs

- **To draw an arc,** get the Arc tool (see page 44), then press-and-drag with it, from one end of the arc to the other. Where you begin and end will be the beginning and end of the arc.

Now, the Arc tool draws according to the settings in the "Arc Segment Tool Options," so if you really need arcs in your project, learn to use this dialog box (okay, you need to be a mathematician to *really* know what the settings are doing, but you can get the gist of it):

1   You *can* open the "Arc Segment Tool Options" dialog box by simply clicking in a document window with the Arc tool, but you don't get the dynamic preview this way.

So instead, first choose the Arc tool so it is visible in the Tools panel (instead of hidden beneath the other tools); now double-click the tool icon in the Tools panel.

2   In the dialog box that appears (shown below), experiment with the settings. When you see the results you want in the live preview pane, click OK.

Proportional width of the arc.

Proportional height of the arc.

This setting determines whether the base of the arc is along the X Axis or the Y Axis. The best thing to do is choose one, see what the preview does, and then experiment on the page.

Arc Segment Tool Options

Length X–Axis: 1 in   OK

Length Y–Axis: 1 in   Cancel

Type: Closed

Base Along: X Axis

Concave   Slope: 50   Convex

Fill Arc

Check this box to fill the arc with the current Fill color. If you don't check it, the Fill is None.

The slope must be between -100 and 100. Instead of entering a number, you can drag the slider.

3   Hold down the Shift key and drag with the Arc tool to constrain the arc to the settings you entered in this dialog box.

You'll notice that if you drag with the Arc tool *without* the Shift key held down, some of the settings hold, but you can easily distort the shape.

The Rectangular Grid tool

The Rectangular Grid tool creates a grid drawn to your specifications. Grids can be used for visual organization or as a decorative design element.

TASK 14 Create a rectangular grid

1 Select the Rectangular Grid tool (it's one of the line tools; see page 44).

2 Click in a document; this opens the "Rectangular Grid Tool Options."

3 To start, use the settings shown below, then click OK.
The grid appears in your document.

4 To change the fill and stroke attributes, use the fill and stroke controls in the Control bar (see page 40, Task 2).

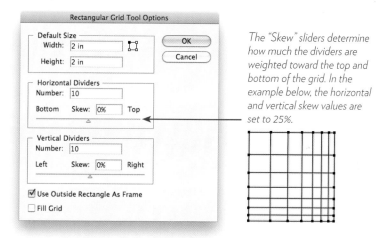

The "Skew" sliders determine how much the dividers are weighted toward the top and bottom of the grid. In the example below, the horizontal and vertical skew values are set to 25%.

• **Alternate method:** Instead of using the "Rectangular Grid Tool Options" dialog box, as described in Steps 1–4, you can select the Rectangular Grid tool and just drag a grid shape on the artboard.

The grid is drawn using the settings in the dialog box above. You can add or remove rows on the fly as you drag a grid.

To add or remove rows as you drag, tap the up or down arrow keys.

To add or remove columns as you drag, tap the left or right arrow keys.

To constrain the grid to a square, hold down the Shift key as you drag.

TIP: If you try to change fill and stroke colors but nothing gets applied—it all just looks like paths— that's because you are in Outline mode. Go to the View menu and choose "Preview."

The Polar Grid tool

The Polar Grid tool draws circular grids, as you can see below, useful for drawing globes, targets for your backyard archery tournament, logos, and even stove burners. Truly, a polar grid really can come in handy. As with all of the Line tools, you can use a Tool Options dialog box to create artwork, or go straight to dragging a shape and using keyboard controls to modify it.

TASK 15   Draw different kinds of polar grids

1 Select the Polar Grid tool (see page 44).

2 Click in a document, which opens the "Polar Grid Tool Options."

3 For now, use the settings shown below, then click OK.
   The specified circular grid appears in your document.

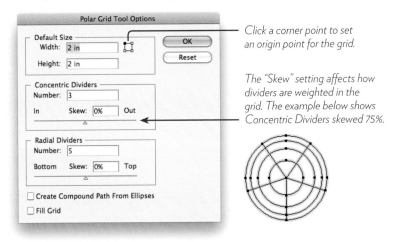

Click a corner point to set an origin point for the grid.

The "Skew" setting affects how dividers are weighted in the grid. The example below shows Concentric Dividers skewed 75%.

4 Now try it without going through the dialog box: Select the Polar Grid tool and drag in the document window.

   Constrain the grid to a circle: Hold down the Shift key as you drag.

   Add or remove concentric dividers: Tap the up or down arrow keys as you drag.

   Add or remove radial dividers: Tap the left or right arrow keys as you drag.

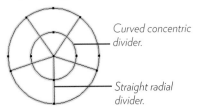

Curved concentric divider.

Straight radial divider.

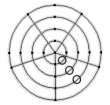

This grid has three concentric dividers and five radial dividers.

Compound paths

We talked about drawing open paths (lines) and closed paths (shapes of all sorts) on page 28. There's another path type that you'll often run across when drawing shapes—a compound path.

A compound path is made of two (or more) overlapping paths, and where they overlap a hole is created in the bottom fill by the shape of the top path. That may sound confusing, but it's easy to do.

TASK 16   Draw a compound path

1 Draw a star shape: Select the Star tool from the Tools panel, then drag a star shape on an artboard (see page 42 if you need more details). Fill it with a color if it isn't already.

2 Now select the Ellipse tool and drag a circle shape (page 41) on top of the star shape.

3 Choose the Selection tool and marquee around both shapes (below).

4 With both shapes selected, choose Object > Compound Path > Make.

A circle-shaped hole is cut out of the star shape (left). A compound path takes on the fill and stroke attributes of the backmost object (the star), and it behaves like a grouped object. When other shapes are behind the compound path, they show through the hole in the compound path. Use the white Direct Selection tool to select individual parts of the compound path.

5 **To release a *selected* compound path,** choose Object > Compound Path > Release.

A background shape shows through the hole in a compound path.

This logo includes a compound path that allows background objects to show through.

Try this!

Using the tools you played with in this chapter and the selection methods you read about in Chapter 3, create a silly face such as the one below. Make an artboard 4 x 6 inches, and use as many tools as you can. In the process of creating even a silly face, you will learn a great deal about the tools, selecting items appropriately, sending objects to the back and bringing others to the front (page 36), and other features of actually producing a product.

Also spend some time in your own discovery mode—check out the options for line strokes and play with some of the color swatches that aren't just flat color (such as the inside of the hole in the letter O, below). Share with others what you discovered.

5 Drawing with Pen and Pencil

The image below is pretty much what my first Pen tool drawing in Illustrator looked like. I was convinced that nothing useful could possibly be done with that crazy thing.

But the Pen tool is Illustrator's primary tool, so you really need to master it. The truth is, you just need to understand a few basic concepts about vector paths and how to manipulate them.

This chapter is filled with Pen (and Pencil) tool tasks that will reveal vector truths and make known the vector path to tranquility and artiness.

Unfamous Quotes:
"What in vector's name is going on here?"
John, 1988

Pen tool basic training

The Pen tool draws a path between clicks. It's that simple. If you just click here and click there, you create a **path** made of straight lines. You can actually create a drawing with simple clicks and straight lines, no curves necessary (below). However, curves add flexibility and accuracy, and are far more efficient (fewer anchor points) than simulating a curve with tiny straight lines.

Even if you've never drawn with the Pen tool before, by the time you complete the following tasks, you will have begun your new journey as a Master of Paths and Points.

NOTE: We suggest you re-read pages 28–29 to refresh your mind about paths, segments, and points before you begin working with the Pen!

TASK 1   Draw an *open path* made of straight segments

Choose the Pen tool from the Tools panel, then use the stroke controls in the Control panel to assign a stroke color and size. Below, I used a 14-point stroke and a tan color from the *Stroke Color* pop-up panel.

1   Click anywhere in a document.

■   An **anchor point** (the small square shown to the left) appears at the point of your click. When an anchor point is selected, it is colored; when an anchor point is not selected, it is white (as shown below).

2   Click semi-randomly in your document, similar to the pattern below. Each time you click, the path extends to that click.

Each time you click, you create a **corner point.**

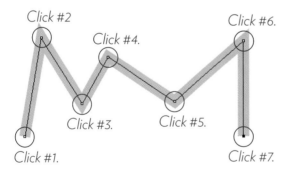

Click #2.
Click #4.
Click #6.
Click #3.
Click #5.
Click #1.
Click #7.

3   **To release the Pen tool from the path,** hold down the Command key (PC: Control key) and click anywhere *except* on the path.

Or choose another tool in the Tools panel.

TASK 2   Draw a *closed path* with curved and straight segments

Chose the Pen tool from the Tools panel, then follow the captions.

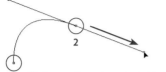

1   Click.

Press here (#2) (don't click) and **drag direction handles** out of the anchor point to create a **smooth point**. As you drag, the line changes depending on the length and the angle at which you drag.

When you release the mouse, the stroke width appears.

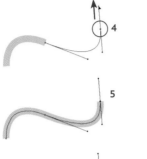

Move the Pen tool to position #4, then **press-and-drag** upward to pull handles out of the anchor point. Again, as you drag, notice how the curved segment changes as you drag the handles to different lengths and at different angles.

When you release the mouse, the stroke appears on the new curved segment; #5.

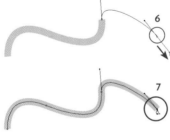

Press in this approximate position (#6) and **drag** downward to pull handles out of the new anchor point.

Now you're going to **change the point you just made** so it will change direction abruptly: **Click** (don't drag) **directly on point #6** to change it (#7); the path now **curves into** the new anchor point, but there is only one handle **exiting** that anchor point. As a result, the next click will cause the path to change directions sharply instead of smoothly (this combination of a corner point and smooth point is called a **cusp point**; see page 56).

Create a **corner point: Click** (don't drag) at the position shown (#8).

To close the path, click directly on the original starting point (#9). The pointer displays a tiny circle next to the Pen icon, indicating that the path will be closed. Make sure you see that tiny circle before you click!

Now you have a **closed path!** Ta da! You are on your way to Greatness.

REMINDER: Single-**click** to create a **corner point** with **no** direction handles.
Press-and-drag to create a **smooth point** with **two** direction handles.

TASK 3 Create a curve in a straight segment with cusp points

A **cusp point** is an anchor point that is a combination of a smooth point and a corner point; that is, it can create a sharp point with either one straight segment and one curved, or with two curved segments. A direction handle appears only toward a curved segment. Also see page 58.

1 Draw a straight path segment (below, left).

2 Hover the Pen tool over the end point, and you see the pointer change to the "Convert Anchor Point" icon (it has a tiny caret symbol, shown below, left).

3 Single-click directly on the end point, and drag a handle out of the point, angled in the direction you want the path to follow (below, center).

4 Position the Pen tool where you want to place the next anchor point (below, right), then click.

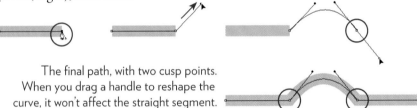

The final path, with two cusp points.
When you drag a handle to reshape the
curve, it won't affect the straight segment.

Essential tasks with the Pen tool

Now that you're comfortable creating a basic path (right?), learn these essential techniques to make the path do just what you need it to do.

TASK 4 Reshape a path

The black Selection tool selects the object as one big piece to move it, as you learned in Chapters 3 and 4. But to **reshape an object**, which is a fundamental task in Illustrator, you'll use the *white* Direct Selection tool.

1 If you don't have either of the paths you created on the previous pages, create a new path now.

2 Choose the white Direct Selection tool.

3 Click on a **smooth point** to get its handles, then drag a handle to **reshape** the curved segments **on both sides** of the anchor point.

4 Click on a **cusp point** to get its handle, then drag that handle to **reshape** just the **curved segment.**

5 Click on a **corner point** (or any point) and drag to reposition the point and the **segments on both sides** of the point.

TASK 5   Add points to a path

After you create a path, you may find that you need to add more anchor points to it so you can make certain modifications.

1   Select the Pen tool and draw a simple open path, as in Task 1.

2   Hover the pointer over any part of a path segment.

The Pen pointer changes to include a plus sign (below, left), a visual clue that a new anchor point will be added at that point when you click.

3   Click the path with the Pen tool (below, left) to add the point. Click on a straight segment and you get a corner point; click on a curved segment and you get a smooth point.

4   Now you can choose the white Direct Selection tool and drag the new anchor point into another position.

TASK 6   Delete points from a path

1   Hover the Pen tool over an anchor point.

The Pen tool icon displays a tiny minus sign (below, left), a visual clue that the anchor point will be deleted when you click it.

2   Click the anchor point. The point is deleted and the path is redrawn.

NOTE: Hidden under the Pen tool in the Tools panel are the "Add Anchor Point Tool" and the "Delete Anchor Point Tool." The Pen tool is smart enough to know which of these tools to automatically switch to when it hovers over a path (to add a point) or an anchor (to delete a point).

As you create art or do other tasks with the Pen tool, you will often find yourself needing to **convert one type of point into another.** Fortunately, this essential operation is easy to do.

TASK 7 Convert a point to another type of point

If you are in the process of drawing the path:

1 Create a short path with several corner points and curve points.

2 Hover the Pen tool over a point (not the end point), and hold down the Option key (PC: Alt key). The pointer changes into the "Convert Anchor Point" icon (below, left).

3 **Corner point to curved point:** Press-and-drag *in the direction in which the path was first drawn* to pull handles out of the point. As you drag, the length and angle of the handles determines the shape of the line segments on each side of the anchor point (below, center).

4 **Curved point to corner point:** Click.

If you just drew a curved point and you want it to be a corner point, click on it. The path will redraw (below, right), then you can carry on from the end of the path to continue drawing.

If you have already created the path and released the Pen tool (as in Task 1.3):

1 First select the path with either Selection tool (black or white).

2 From the Tools panel, choose the "Convert Anchor Point Tool" (it's with the other hidden Pen tools).

3 Position the pointer over the point you want to convert.

Corner point to curved point: Press-and-drag *in the direction in which the path was first drawn.*

Curved point to corner point: Click.

TIP: While you're using the Pen tools, tear off a floating panel of all the tools so they are easily accessible—see page 16.

If you only learn to create corner point and curve points, you will get frustrated when working on a project. **Cusp points** (a combination of sharp corners and curves) are fundamental to the drawing process, so spend a few minutes to learn how to convert other points to cusps (in addition to Task 3, in which you create cusp points as you draw).

TASK 8   Convert a smooth point into a cusp point that connects two curved segments with a sharp point

The advantage of this kind of point is that the handles on the cusp point allow you to adjust just one segment of the curve at a time, each independent of the other.

1   Create a path with a few curve points in it.

2   With the white Direct Selection tool, click on a curve point to select it and display its handles (below, left).

3   Choose the "Convert Anchor Point Tool" from the Tools panel (it's with the other hidden Pen tools), and drag one of the direction points on the end of a handle in any direction (below, right).

4   Now that the point is converted, you can use the white Direct Selection tool to drag either handle independently.

New cusp point with two handles that operate independently.

TASK 9   Convert a point into a cusp point connecting a straight segment with a curved segment

If you are in the process of drawing the path:

1   With the Pen tool, hover over the point and hold down the Option key (PC: Alt key) to get the "Convert Anchor Point" tool.

2   Press-and-drag on the point to pull out handles. Now, *keep the Option/Alt key down* so you still have the "Convert Anchor Point" tool, and drag one of the handles back into the point.

3   Let go of the Option/Alt key and continue drawing from the end point.

If you have already created the path and released the Pen tool:

1   With the white Direct Selection tool, click on the point to select it and display its handles.

2   Drag one of the handles all the way back into the point.

TASK 10 Reposition an anchor point as you draw

1 Draw a straight path segment (below, left).

2 *Press* (don't click) to create an end point, *plus* hold down the Spacebar, then drag the end point to another position (below). As long as you hold down the Spacebar, you can drag the anchor to other positions.

3 When the end point is in the position you want it, let go of the Spacebar and continue drawing.

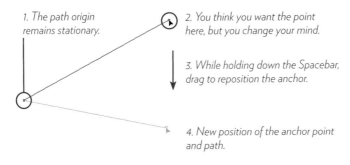

1. The path origin remains stationary.

2. You think you want the point here, but you change your mind.

3. While holding down the Spacebar, drag to reposition the anchor.

4. New position of the anchor point and path.

TASK 11 Assign a brush stroke to a path

This technique works no matter which tool you use to draw a path—the Pen tool, Pencil tool, or the various Shape tools.

1 Create a path of any sort (below, left). Make sure it is selected.

2 Open the Brushes panel: Choose Window > Brushes (below, center).

3 Click the "Chalk-Scribble" thumbnail, shown below.

There are other great brush libraries to choose from: Click the *Brush Libraries Menu* button in the bottom-left corner of the Brushes panel, then choose a library from the list. See Chapter 6 for more details.

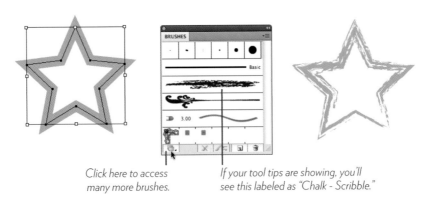

Click here to access many more brushes.

If your tool tips are showing, you'll see this labeled as "Chalk - Scribble."

Drawing with the Pencil tool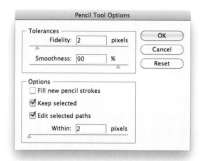

Drawing with the Pencil tool is similar to drawing with a real pencil, with the advantage of being able to add degrees of smoothing to strokes. It also has the disadvantage of being pretty dang unpredictable, so it's not our favorite drawing tool. But when you need a slightly primitive, hand-drawn effect or handlettering, the Pencil tool is fast and easy.

The Pencil tool automatically adds anchor points as determined by the settings in the "Pencil Tool Options" dialog box, so review this box before drawing.

TASK 12   Set your Pencil tool options

1   Double-click the Pencil tool icon in the Tools panel to open the options.

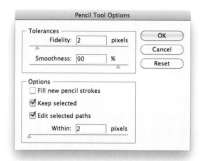

2   Adjust the "Tolerances" settings:

> **Fidelity** determines how far the pencil moves before adding an anchor point. A higher value creates a smoother, less complex path.
>
> **Smoothness** controls the amount of automatic smoothing applied to a stroke. A higher value creates more smoothing.

3   Choose the items you want to activate in the "Options" section:

> **Fill new pencil strokes:** When this item is selected, paths are filled with the current fill color as you draw them. This doesn't mean only *closed* paths: It draws an imaginary line from end point to end point and fills any spaces with the currently chosen fill color. Try it to see what I mean.
>
> **Keep selected:** When you finish drawing a path, the path stays selected so you can modify it.
>
> **Edit selected paths:** This determines how close your mouse or stylus must be to a path in order to edit the path with the Pencil tool (see the following page). Set the distance you prefer with the slider.

4   Click OK.

TASK 13 Draw a star with the Pencil tool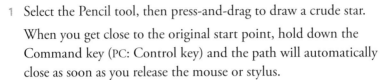

1 Select the Pencil tool, then press-and-drag to draw a crude star.

When you get close to the original start point, hold down the Command key (PC: Control key) and the path will automatically close as soon as you release the mouse or stylus.

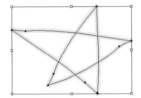

Shaky lines will smooth themselves automatically when you release the pointer.

When you hold down the Command/Control key, the Pencil tool pointer displays a small circle to indicate the path will close.

When you release the pointer, the path closes, and the stroke is considerably smoother (below) than the original path (above) led you to believe (assuming you changed the options as shown on the previous page).

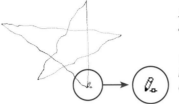

2 Now use the Pencil tool **to modify the path.** This seems kind of weird, but it actually works.

With the white Direct Selection tool, select the star path.

With the Pencil tool, draw a revised path on one of the star arms (as in the example below, left)—start and end the drag on top of an existing path. When you release the mouse or stylus, the path is redrawn and smoothness is applied again (below, center).

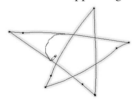

3 **Change the stroke width, and the caps and joins:** Open the Stroke panel and experiment (see pages 64–66). Turn the stroke into a dashed line, or apply a different stroke profile.

Also **add a color fill:** In the Control panel, click the *Fill Color* pop-up menu (see page 40) and choose a color swatch.

TASK 14   Smooth the path

The Smooth tool makes paths smoother. The degree to which it smooths is determined by settings in the "Smooth Tool Options" dialog box, which are the same as the "Tolerances" settings as explained on page 61.

1   Double-click the Pencil tool or the Smooth tool to get the options.

2   In the "Tolerances" settings, higher values result in smoother paths. Try different settings as you experiment with Steps 3 and 4.

3   Create a path. It can be a path created with the Pen tool or the Pencil tool, but Pencil tool paths are more likely to need smoothing.

4   Drag the Smooth tool along a path you want to smooth. The drag doesn't have to be exactly on top of the path, as shown below.

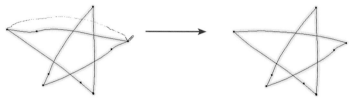

Drag the Smooth tool along the path you want to smooth; be sure the start and end points of the drag touch the path.

Dragging the Smooth tool on top of a path, above it, or below it, will create different results.

Try this: *Drag the Smooth tool from a path toward the direction you want the path to bend to, as shown above.*

Smooth tool results are unpredictable, but it worked this time.

TASK 15   Erase bits of a path

Drag the Path Eraser tool (find it under the Pencil tool) along a path (below, left), or from one section of a path to another (below, right).

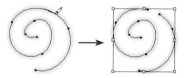
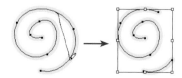

Erase a small section of a path.

Erase a large section of a path.

Customize strokes with the Stroke panel

The Stroke panel provides essential controls and options for customizing strokes on both closed and open paths.

TASK 16 Use the Stroke panel to customize paths

1 **To open the Strokes panel**, do one of the following:
   - Click the word "Stroke" in the Control panel.
   - Choose Window > Stroke.
   - If the Stroke panel is docked in the vertical dock on the side of your workspace (with other panels), click its icon.

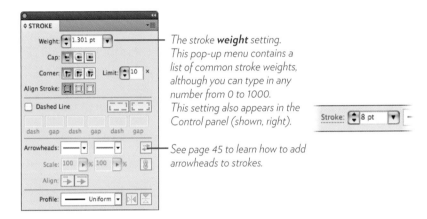

The stroke **weight** setting. This pop-up menu contains a list of common stroke weights, although you can type in any number from 0 to 1000. This setting also appears in the Control panel (shown, right).

See page 45 to learn how to add arrowheads to strokes.

2 **Draw an open path**, similar to the one below. Select the path, and use the Stroke panel to make the settings in the following steps.

3 **Select a stroke "Weight":** Choose a line thickness from the "Weight" pop-up menu, *or* type a number in the value field.

4 **Choose a "Cap" style:** This setting determines how the end point of a stroke is drawn. The buttons, left to right, are "Butt Cap," "Round Cap," and "Projecting Cap."

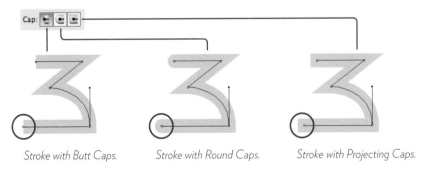

Stroke with Butt Caps.   *Stroke with Round Caps.*   *Stroke with Projecting Caps.*

5 **Choose a "Corner" style:** This setting affects the appearance of the stroke where two path segments join. The buttons, left to right are "Miter Join," "Round Join," and "Bevel Join." Try all three.

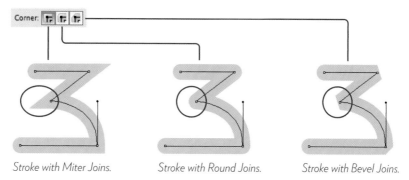

Stroke with Miter Joins.   *Stroke with Round Joins.*   *Stroke with Bevel Joins.*

6 **Change the stroke alignment of a closed path:** Use the Rectangle tool to draw a closed path, then click the "Align Stroke" buttons to change how the stroke is applied to the shape's path. As you see below, the alignment you choose actually changes the size of the shape.

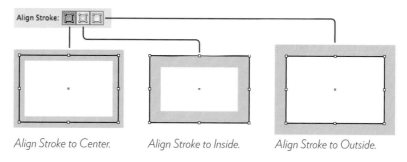

Align Stroke to Center.   *Align Stroke to Inside.*   *Align Stroke to Outside.*

7 **Change a solid stroke to a "Dashed Line":** Select a closed or open path, then check the "Dashed Line" box.

Click here to automatically size dashes to align perfectly with ends and corners, rather than preserving exact dash and gap values.

Try different "dash" and "gap" values. Also experiment with different Cap styles, explained on the opposite page. And then choose a different "Profile" for the line, as shown on the next page! Oh my!

The "Cap" setting for this stroke is "Round Cap."

The "Cap" setting for this stroke is "Butt Cap."

—continued

8 **Apply a different "Profile,"** which changes the shape of a stroke: Select a path, and make sure it's got a nice, fat stroke on it. Click the "Profile" pop-up menu to display a scrolling list of profile thumbnails to choose from. Experiment with selecting different profiles.

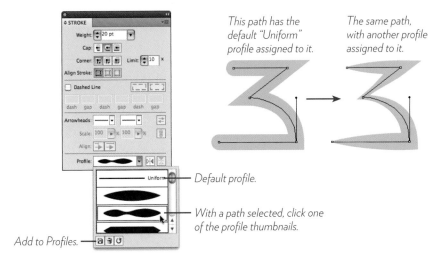

This path has the default "Uniform" profile assigned to it.

The same path, with another profile assigned to it.

Default profile.

With a path selected, click one of the profile thumbnails.

Add to Profiles.

TASK 17   Create a custom stroke profile

Omigosh, you can even customize a stroke, then save it as a profile to be used later! The possibilities are truly infinite.

1 Draw a path and modify it with the Width tool (see page 47).

A 30-point stroke, modified with the Width tool.

2 While that stroke is *selected,* click the *Add to Profiles* button in the bottom-left corner of the Profile scrolling list (called out, above-left).

3 Name the profile, then click OK.

4 The new profile now appears in the pop-up menu and can be applied to strokes at any time.

The new custom profile is assigned to an existing path.

Try this!

The Pen tool is the heart and soul of Illustrator. Because of its importance, we've added extra practice sessions so you can really become comfortable with it. We guarantee (pretty much) that if you do all the tasks in this chapter, plus these additional exercises, you will feel amazingly competent with the Pen tool, and thus amazingly competent in Illustrator.

These tasks involve tracing over an existing image, in this case, letters. Not only will this process confirm your expertise with the Pen tool, but you'll learn a valuable technique (tracing) that you can apply to many projects.

TASK 18   Create a layer for tracing

1   Choose the Text tool.

2   In the Control panel, set the character to "Times New Roman," the style to "Bold," and the size to 300 points.

3   Click on an artboard and type the letter O.

4   Change the letter's fill color to light gray: Select the O, click the *Fill Color* pop-up panel in the Control panel, and choose a light-gray color swatch (see page 40).

5   Open the Layers panel (Window > Layers) and *lock* the layer that contains the letter O: Click the box to the left of the layer name to put a lock icon in it, as shown below. This is your template.

6   Create a new drawing layer *on top of* the existing layer: Click the *Create New Layer* icon at the bottom of the Layers panel.

Select this new layer (if it isn't already), and carry on with the next Task.

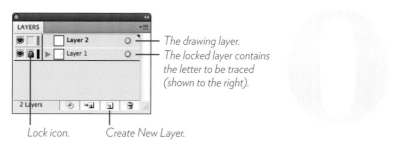

The drawing layer.
The locked layer contains the letter to be traced (shown to the right).

Lock icon.   Create New Layer.

TASK 19 Trace the letter O with the Pen tool

We're starting with the letter O because (ideally) a circular shape like this should have only four points, one on each extremity. As you trace over the letter and try to make the strokes line up exactly, you will get a good feel for how to adjust the points as you draw.

1 Choose the Pen tool, then set these options in the Control panel: a *Fill Color* of *None,* a colored stroke (your choice), a 1-point weight, a "Uniform" profile, and the "Basic" brush definition, as shown below.

2 Position the Pen tool at the top-center of the shape.

Press (don't click) to create an anchor point, and continue to press as you drag handles out of the anchor point, to the right (as shown below). Hold down the Shift key to keep the handles perfectly horizontal.

When the right handle is the length of about a third of the way to the midpoint on the side of the O, let go.

Drag handles in a clockwise manner to draw a path.

(If you prefer to work in a counterclockwise manner, you can do that.)

3 Position the Pen tool at midpoint on the right side of the shape (circled in #2 on the opposite page), then press-and-drag handles out of the anchor point. Hold down the Shift key to keep the handles perfectly vertical as you drag to match the shape of the O.

4 Click at the midpoint of the bottom side and Shift-drag handles out of the anchor point, until the path matches the O shape (#3 on the opposite page).

5 Click at the midpoint of the left side, then Shift-drag handles out until the path matches the O shape (#4 on the opposite page).

To create a smooth curve, try to make each handle cover about a third of the curved path between anchor points.

If the angle between a handle and the curve is similar on both ends of the curve, it will be smoother and more symmetrical.

6   Position the Pen tool over the original start point. A small circle appears next to the Pen tool cursor (below, left) to let you know if you click there, it will close the path.

7   Press-and-drag handles out of the final anchor until the path matches the O shape (below, center). If necessary, use the techniques you learned in this chapter to adjust the shape.

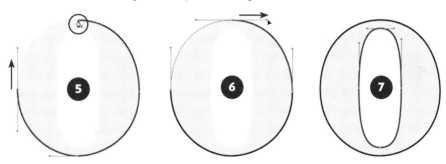

8   Repeat Steps 2–5 for the inner circle. The result should look like the letter shown above, right.

9   Hide the O layer to see how lovely your traced letterform is: Click the eyeball icon for that layer in the Layers panel.

10 Convert the two shapes into a compound path (page 51) or the letter won't have a hole in the middle: Select both shapes, then choose Object > Compound Path > Make.

11 Go to the Control panel and choose a color from the *Color Fill* pop-up panel. Et voilà!

Fill pop-up panel.

And try this!

In this exercise, draw the letter Q. Instead of being made up completely of curves, it includes a couple of corner points and cusp points. Bwahahaha.

TASK 20 Trace the letter Q with the Pen tool

Follow the steps in Task 18 on page 67 to set up a locked layer for tracing, but type a giant letter Q instead of O. Follow the steps in Task 19.1 to set the options for the Pen tool.

1 Position the Pen tool at the top-center of the shape. *Press* (don't click) to create an anchor point, and continue to press as you drag handles out of the anchor point, to the right (as shown below). Hold down the Shift key to keep the handles perfectly horizontal.

2 Position the Pen tool at the midpoint of the right side of the shape (circled, below-center), then press-and-drag handles out of the anchor point until the path matches the Q shape.

3 Place the Pen tool at the position shown in #3, then press-and-drag handles out of the anchor point until the path matches the shape.

4 Hover the Pen tool over the point you just made; a tiny caret symbol appears next to the pen, indicating it is going to change the identity of that point. Single-click directly on that point you just made; the outgoing handle disappears (#4, below). This is now a cusp point.

5 Press-and-drag to set a point at the end of the tail shape, shaping the path to match the Q shape.

6 As in Step 4, click the anchor point to remove the outgoing handle.

7 *Click* the bottom corner of the tail—don't drag. The next path needs to come abruptly (not smoothly) out of that anchor point.

8 Press-and-drag to set a point at the left side of the tail where it meets the oval shape of the letter, shaping the path to match the tail (#8).

9 Click the anchor point just created, to remove the handle coming out of it and force the next path to exit the anchor point abruptly.

10 Position the Pen tool at the midway point of the Q's left side, then press-and-drag upward (hold down the Shift key) to bring handles out of the anchor point; shape the curve to match the Q (#10).

11 Position the Pen tool over the original start point, then press-and-drag handles out of the anchor point until the path matches the Q shape. This closes the path. Ta da!

12 Use the Pen tool to draw the inside oval shape, as you did on page 69.

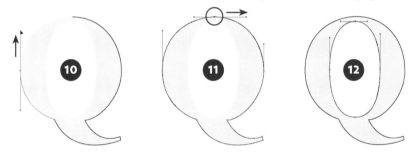

13 Select both shapes, then choose Object > Compound Path > Make (if you don't, your Q won't have a hole in the middle).

14 Select the compound path, go to the Control panel, and choose a color from the *Color Fill* pop-up panel. Hey, now try an S!

*Color Fill pop-up panel
in the Control panel.*

TIP: Every now and then, remember to hide the Q layer (click its eyeball icon in the Layers panel) so you can see how your shape is progressing.

And try this too!

This exercise will make you more familiar with the Pencil tool and with tracing templates—and it's a little more fun than tracing a Q. This task uses the Pencil tool, and you will learn that the secret to Pencil tool success is in Task 22.

A tracing template fades out the image that's on it so you can trace over it. You can only put raster images on a tracing template, so you'll need a raster image of some sort to trace from—something you've scanned or drawn on paper or borrowed from the web just to use as an exercise. Maybe a big bug or a flower.

TASK 21   Prepare to trace from a template

1   Place an image in an Illustrator document: Locate any raster image file (JPEG or TIFF is best) on your computer and drag it into an open document window. *Or* choose File > Place… to find and place a file in your open Illustrator document.

2   Open the Layers panel: Choose Window > Layers. You'll see that the placed image is on its own layer in the Layers panel.

3   Open the "Layer Options" dialog box: In the Layers panel, double-click the layer that contains the placed image. You'll get this dialog box:

The image on the tracing template will be dim, and you can draw on top of it on another layer.

4   In the "Layer Options," click the "Template" box.

By default, the "Dim Images" value is set to 50%, but we prefer a setting between 20 and 30%.

Click OK. The layer is now a *template* layer and the image is dimmed.

5   Create a *new* layer above the template layer to draw on: Click the *Create New Layer* icon at the bottom of the Layers panel (shown below).

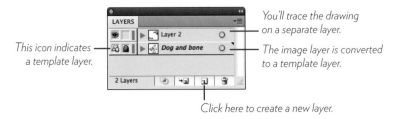

This icon indicates a template layer.

You'll trace the drawing on a separate layer.

The image layer is converted to a template layer.

Click here to create a new layer.

TASK 22   Get your Pencil tool ready

1   Set some defaults before you start to draw: Double-click the Pencil tool in the Tools panel to open the "Pencil Tool Options."

Copy the settings you see here.

For accurate tracing, automatic smoothing is a problem. Set the "Tolerance" values very low, as shown here.

Deselect "Keep selected" to prevent new pencil strokes from joining or reshaping the previous stroke.

2   Now open the Stroke panel (choose Window > Stroke, or click the word "Stroke" in the Control panel) to set some stroke defaults.

Choose a stroke weight of 3 points, a "Round Cap," and set the "Corner" option to "Round Join."

Set stroke weight.

Cap and Corner settings (pages 64–65).

Now you're ready to start tracing your image!

TASK 23   Trace the template image

1   Choose the Pencil tool. On the new layer you created, start tracing the image that you can see from the dim template layer.

The dimmed image is on the template layer. When you're ready to turn off the visibility of the original image, click the template icon on the left side of the layer (where the eyeball usually is).

—continued

The finished tracing doesn't have as much character as it could because all the strokes are uniform—and boring. To be less of a bore, follow Steps 2 and 3.

2   Select all the paths in the drawing (Select > All).

3   Assign a different stroke profile: Open the Stroke panel, then from the "Profile" pop-up menu shown below, choose a preset profile (other than the default "Uniform" profile). (See page 66 for details about stroke profiles.)

The line variation created by the "Width Profile 2" setting makes the drawing look less mechanical and more like a real pen and ink drawing.

4   For a final refinement, I chose certain strokes and assigned another profile to them. I also modified a few strokes that seemed too thin by thickening them with the Width tool (see Chapter 7 for information about the amazing Width tool).

6 Vector Brushes

In addition to the other amazing drawing tools (shapes, pen, pencil, lines), Illustrator provides lots of different brush tools.

Most of Illustrator's brushes are what we describe as *path* brushes; they draw vector paths to which you can assign different brush effects. These include Calligraphic Brushes, Scatter Brushes, Art Brushes, Bristle Brushes, and Pattern Brushes. If you want to change a brush effect, just select the path and choose another effect. This chapter discusses the most commonly used ones.

The Blob brush, however, doesn't create a *path* like the other brushes; it draws brush *shapes* that are filled with color. This brush has some unique characteristics that make it a particularly powerful and fun tool to use.

Vector brushes

Most of the brushes in Illustrator are *brush effects* that are assigned to *paths*. You can apply brush effects to existing paths, or select a brush effect and then create a path for it. The Brushes panel shows you a sampling of the different types of path-based brushes (which doesn't include the Blob brush).

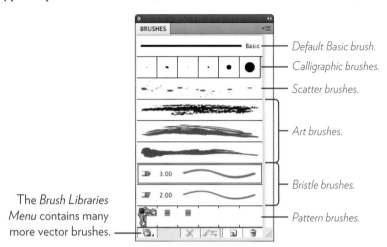

Default Basic brush.

Calligraphic brushes.

Scatter brushes.

Art brushes.

Bristle brushes.

The *Brush Libraries Menu* contains many more vector brushes.

Pattern brushes.

TASK 1 Add brushes to the Brushes panel

Add different brush effects to the Brushes panel before you start playing so you have lots to choose from.

1 To open the Brushes panel, choose Window > Brushes.

2 Click the *Brush Libraries Menu* in the bottom-left corner of the panel, then choose a library. It opens in its own floating panel.

3 **Click a brush in the chosen library panel to make it appear in the Brushes panel.**

Once a brush is in the Brushes panel, you can double-click its thumbnail to open its "Brush Options" where you can adjust its specific settings, such as diameter (size), roundness, and angle.

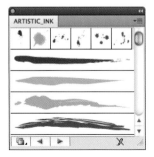

Artistic_Ink is one of the "Artistic" brush libraries.

TASK 2   Apply artistic brush strokes to paths

You can apply brush effects from different libraries to existing paths. *Or* you can first select a brush effect from a library, and then draw a path with that effect using the Paintbrush tool.

Apply a brush effect to an existing stroke

1   Select an existing stroke that you created in a previous task (below, left), or draw one now (the spiral brush, as used in the example below, is explained on pages 46–47) and make sure it is selected.

2   Open the Brushes panel (Window > Brushes).

3   Open a brush library: Click the *Brush Libraries* menu in the bottom-left corner of the Brushes panel, then choose a library.

4   In the floating panel of the library that you chose, select one of the brush thumbnails.

The effect is applied to the selected path, shown below-right.

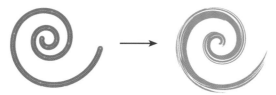

This is the "Dry Ink 1" brush from the Artistic Ink brush library, applied to an existing spiral path.

TIP: If you selected a brush effect and nothing happened to your path, that's because the **path** wasn't selected. Make sure to select it, then try again.

Choose a brush effect *first,* and *then* draw a path

1   Follow Steps 2–4, above (except the effect will not be applied yet).

2   Choose the Paintbrush tool. Make sure nothing on the page is selected.

3   From the Control panel, choose a stroke weight of at least 6 points, and choose a stroke color. If there is a color fill chosen, change it to None.

4   Drag to create paths, such as the handlettering shown below.

I used the Fountain Pen brush. Because an effect like this starts out blobby and gets thinner, you can draw "backwards," as in the second R, to put the blobs somewhere else besides at the beginning.

TASK 3 Explore the Calligraphic brushes

Calligraphic brushes are styled after the brushes used in calligraphy, the art of decorative handwriting. Calligraphy brushes and pens are usually flat and held at an angle to produce strokes with pronounced variations in the thicks and thins of the letterforms.

1   In the bottom-left corner of the Brushes panel, click the *Brush Libraries* icon, choose "Artistic," then choose "Artistic_Calligraphic."

2   Choose one of the brush tip thumbnails in the "Artistic_Calligraphic" panel, as shown below. When you choose a calligraphy brush from a library, its icon is added to the top of the Brushes panel.

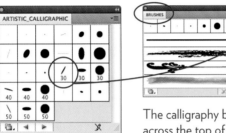

To set options for a brush effect, *double-click its thumbnail in the Brushes panel.*

The calligraphy brushes line up in a row across the top of the Brushes panel.

3   Choose the Paintbrush tool, then draw the numerals 1, 2, and 3, as shown below. Depending on the brush tip you chose, the settings you gave it, and how you draw the numbers, your calligraphy surely looks very different from this example (yours probably looks better, darn it).

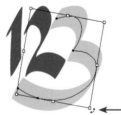

A brush path is editable. Use the black or white selection tools (as appropriate) to change its color, distort its shape, resize it, etc.

To rotate a brush path: *Select a path with the black Selection tool. Hover the pointer near a corner; when the pointer changes into the "rotate" symbol, as shown here, drag in a circular motion.*

4   If your drawn numbers aren't as smooth as you would like, change their smoothness settings (the Paintbrush or the Pencil tool). This doesn't smooth the *existing* stroke—it only affects the strokes you are *going* to draw.

To smooth the settings, double-click the tool in the Tools panel to open its "Tool Options" dialog box. Change the "Tolerance" settings to larger values (larger equals smoother).

TASK 4   Edit existing brush effects

The brush effects act as style sheets in that you can edit the effect at any time *and the results are automatically applied to all strokes in the document that use that effect.* You can choose to have the edits apply only to new strokes if you don't want to affect the ones on the page, but it's important to understand this powerful feature so it doesn't surprise you!

Apply new brush settings to all existing strokes

1   Apply a brush effect to several strokes, as explained in previous tasks.

2   In the Brushes panel, double-click the thumbnail of the effect you used in Step 1. This opens a "Brush Options" dialog box, as shown below. Experiment with the options; click the "Preview" button to see the effects on the page. Be sure to give it a name so you can find it again.

3   When you click OK, you are asked if you want to apply these changes to existing brush strokes. *This does not mean to existing brush strokes that are selected, but to every stroke in the document that uses this effect.* If you don't want that to happen, choose "Leave Strokes," and the changes you made are added to the Brushes panel as a new effect, but nothing on the page, even if it was selected, is changed.

Edit just one object that has a brush effect applied

•   Select a path or paths, then click the *Options of Selected Object* button at the bottom of the Brushes panel (shown below).

A limited version of the "Brush Options" dialog box opens. Change any settings you like, click OK, and the changes are applied only to that path (or paths) that were *selected.*

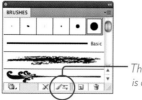

This button, Options of Selected Object, *is dim and unavailable until you select an object.*

TASK 5   Apply a brush effect to text

For a unique text effect, apply brush effects to text. This works best on
large text, such as headlines and display type.

1   With the Type tool, create and format a line of text, such as your
    name (see Chapter 10 to learn all about creating text).

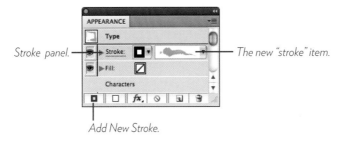

*This is the font Ophir. I set it
in Illustrator at 120-point and
colored it dark brown.*

2   With the black Selection tool, select the text.

3   Open the Appearance panel (Window > Appearance).

4   In the Appearance panel, click the *Add New Stroke* button
    in the bottom-left corner of the panel (shown below).

Stroke panel. ────

The new "stroke" item.

Add New Stroke.

5   Open the Brushes panel and choose a brush effect.

*I applied the Fountain Pen brush effect to the new stroke, and also assigned a green
color to the stroke, using the Appearance panel. Thus you can see the brown
of the text and the green of the stroke.*

*While the text is selected with the black Selection tool and you are trying different
strokes, **the text will appear in a highlight color.** Don't worry—when you deselect
the text, the color you assigneds will reappear.*

If you don't like the effect, try other brushes until you like the
results. You can choose brushes from the Brushes panel, or from any
open brush library panel, or from the Stroke pop-up menu in the
Appearance panel (above).

You can also change the text at any time, its point size, color, font, etc.
Use the Type tool to make those changes.

6 **To change settings for that stroke,** double-click a stroke thumbnail in the Brushes panel (but see the previous page to understand what it will do). Click the "Preview" checkbox to see live updates of the effect as you experiment with different settings.

7 You may need to change the fill or stroke color to get results you like.

The fill color affects the text: To change the fill color, you must select the text with the Type tool, and *then* change its color. (Experiment with a fill color of None so all you see is the stroke.)

The stroke color affects the brush effect that's applied to the text: To change the stroke color, select the text with the black Selection tool, then choose a different effect or double-click on the brush effect in the Brushes panel.

This is the font Schmelvetica, in green, with the brush effect called Fire Ash, colored purple.

This is an ornament from the font Lady Rene. I applied the "Light Wash - Thin" brush effect to it, which I customized (as on page 79) as much thinner than the default. I also lightened the opacity of the stroke a bit, using the option in the Control panel.

TASK 6   Preview various brush effects

1   Draw a path with any tool. I used the Paintbrush tool to draw the numeral 5 in the example below.

2   Select the path with either the white or black Selection tool.

3   Choose a brush from a brush library panel or from the Brushes panel. The path updates immediately to show the applied brush effect.

4   Click again on another brush effect. The selected object discards the previous brush effect and displays the current one. You can preview as many effects as you like in this way.

One object with different calligraphic brushes applied to it.

5   **To remove a brush effect from a stroke,** select the stroke, then click the "Remove Brush Stroke" icon at the bottom of the Brushes menu.

Remove brush stroke from selected object.

6   Every time you click a brush to see how it looks when applied to the selected object, the brush is automatically added to the Brushes panel. After you spend a while previewing effects, you'll have more brushes in your Brushes panel than you want.

To remove unwanted brushes from the Brushes panel, select them, then click the Trash button in the bottom-right corner of the panel.

To remove all brush effects you haven't used, go to the Brushes panel menu and choose, "Select All Unused." Now click on the Trash icon.

TIP: When you add a brush stroke effect to text, the text is still editable. When you add effects to paths, the path is still editable, and you can change the effect at any time.

In Illustrator, you can achieve effects that are not possible otherwise and that you never even thought you could create. The production of random effects can create interesting surprises and help develop many creative solutions to design projects.

TASK 7   Take arrows to a new level

How long do you think it takes to create an arrow/spaghetti illustration like the one below? The correct answer is *thirty seconds or less,* because the Brushes Library Menu includes an Arrows Library collection. But seriously, unique and beautiful arrows can be useful design tools.

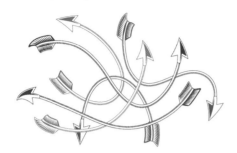
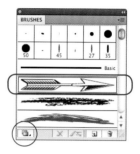

1   In the Brushes panel, click the *Brush Libraries Menu* button in the bottom-left corner. Choose "Arrows," then choose "Arrows_Special"; a floating panel of arrows appears.

2   Click the arrow style you want to use. It appears in the Brushes panel (shown above, right).

3   Select the Paintbrush tool in the Tools panel, then drag to draw a path of any shape. When you release the mouse, the arrow style you selected stretches the length of the path.

You can also *apply* an arrow stroke to paths drawn with the Pen tool, the Pencil tool, the Line Segment tool, and even the shape tools.

If the arrow curves aren't as smooth as you'd like, double-click the Paintbrush tool or the Pencil tool in the Tools panel and change the "Tolerances" settings to larger values. Then draw again.

4   To add color to *selected* arrow paths, click the *Stroke Color* pop-up panel in the Control panel and choose a color swatch.

TASK 8   Create your own arrow brush

A wacky new arrow.

1   Create a long, narrow, artsy arrow.

2   Drag the art into the Brushes panel. In the dialog box that opens, choose "Art Brush."

3   With the new custom art brush selected in the Brushes panel, choose the Paintbrush tool in the Tools panel, then drag to draw arrows.

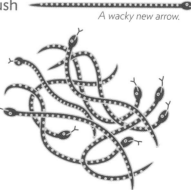

TASK 9 Throw paint on the screen with your custom brush

As if the built-in options weren't enough, you can make a brush out of anything and then use it to throw paint around. Here's one example, and then take yourself on a Discovery Tour to uncover more possibilities!

1   Select the Pencil tool in the Tools panel and draw a horizontal, scribbly shape. Use the default black stroke and no fill color (below, left).

2   Swap the Fill and Stroke colors: Press Shift X (below, right).

3   Drag the black shape into the Brushes panel.

4   In the "New Brush" dialog box that opens (below), select "Art Brush," then click OK.

5   In the "Art Brush Options" dialog box that opens, name the brush stroke and experiment with the various settings (below).

The preview pane shows how the settings affect the stroke.

To enable you to recolor the stroke later, make this change: In the "Colorization" section, click the "Method" pop-up menu and choose "Hue Shift."

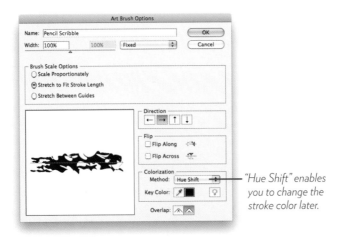

"Hue Shift" enables you to change the stroke color later.

6 Click ᴏᴋ. A thumbnail for the new brush stroke is added to the Brushes panel (shown below).

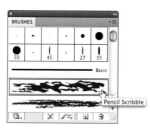

Modify a brush's settings at any time: Double-click a stroke thumbnail to open the "Art Brush Options" for that stroke (but read page 79 first).

Hover the pointer over a thumbnail to show the brush name.

7 With the new brush stroke selected in the Brushes panel, choose the Paintbrush tool.

Draw a curvy path (or any kind of path). The new brush stroke effect is applied to the path.

8 Draw a star with the Star tool (hidden under the Rectangle tool), then while it is still selected, choose the new brush effect.

Draw a shape with the Ellipse tool (also hidden under the Rectangle tool). Select it (if it isn't already) and choose the new brush effect.

You can always (even next week or next year) select the path and change the stroke, color, brush options, etc.

These shapes have a "Width" setting of 50% in the "Art Brush Options" dialog box (shown on the opposite page).

The same ellipse, with a "Width" setting of 100%.

The same ellipse, with a "Width" setting of 175%.

NOTE: Calligraphy (and just about any drawing task) is approximately one gazillion times easier if you use **a pressure-sensitive tablet.** The difference is *dramatic.* Drawing with a mouse (or even with your finger on a trackpad) is extremely challenging, so ***do not*** judge your ability to draw in Illustrator based on how well you draw with a mouse.

TASK 10   Splatter art shapes with the Scatter brush

Scatter brushes use vector artwork objects as paint and splatter multiples of them on a path. You control the effect with your settings in the "Scatter Brush Options" dialog box.

1   In the Brushes panel, click the *Brush Libraries Menu* button in the bottom-left corner, then choose Decorative > Decorative_Scatter.

Single-click the "Star 3" preset in the Decorative_Scatter panel (below, left) to place that selection in the Brushes panel (below, right).

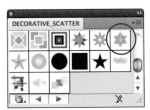 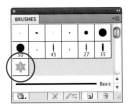

2   Choose the Paintbrush tool and draw a path. The "Star 3" brush effect is applied to the path (below).

The default settings for the "Star 3" brush are set to "Fixed," meaning there is no variation in the star sizes, spacing, scatter, or rotations, as you can see in the example. But you can change that.

3   To change the "Star 3" brush settings, double-click the brush thumbnail in the Brushes panel to open the "Scatter Brush Options."

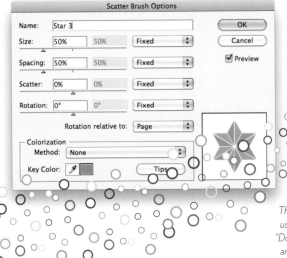

These fun bubbles are one brush swipe using the "Decorative Scatter" brush called "Dot Rings." Notice how some of the rings are opaque and some transparent.

4 Click the "Preview" checkbox so you can see the effect of the changes as you make them. Change any of the "Fixed" options to "Random." This gives each slider two control knobs instead of just one.

Experiment and adjust the attribute sliders until you like the results, then click OK. Draw again with the Paintbrush.

TASK 11   Create your own Scatter brush

In addition to the many preset brushes available, you can create your own brush with your own artwork.

1 Select an art object (below I used the face that you'll create with the Blob brush later in this chapter). Marquee around the object to make sure all paths are selected, then drag the object into the Brushes panel.

2 Select the Paintbrush tool and draw a path. Your object fills the path. To modify how the Scatter Brush renders the artwork on a path, follow the instructions in the previous Task 10, Steps 3 and 4.

TASK 12   Modify an existing art brush

1 Choose the Star 3 brush (from Task 10) and drag it out of the Brushes panel, into your document.

2 Assign different colors to the shapes in the star, then drag the artwork back into the Brushes panel.

3 Select the Paintbrush tool, then draw a path. The modified brush shape is applied to new paths as you draw them.

TASK 13 Expand a brush path to customize the art

After you create a brush stroke along a path, you might want to modify just part of the path. But the artwork that's assigned to a path is not editable until you *expand* the path.

When you expand a path, the artwork on the path is converted to outlines and the path itself is removed and can no longer be manipulated. The shape (or shapes) that populate the path, however, are now fully editable.

1   Use the black Selection tool to select a brush path, such as one of the star Scatter Brush paths you made on page 86.

2   Choose Object > Expand Appearance.

The editable path itself disappears, and the shape (or shapes) assigned to the former path are now editable.

3   Use the white Direct Selection tool to select individual shapes. You can change the colors, select specific anchor points or direction handles to alter a shape's appearance, enlarge or reduce their individual sizes, move them around, etc.

The Blob brush

Indescribable . . . indestructible! Once you start using it you can't stop! Actually, this brush is kinda freaky. It draws blobby *shapes* (not paths) that have a fill and *no* stroke. If you draw on top of another shape that has the same fill color (and no stroke), the top brush stroke is merged with the existing, underlying shape.

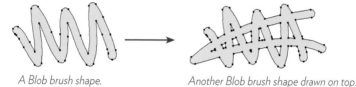

A Blob brush shape.   Another Blob brush shape drawn on top.

The Blob brush works great with a pressure-sensitive tablet—you can apply pressure to vary the stroke widths, which creates a nice calligraphic effect.

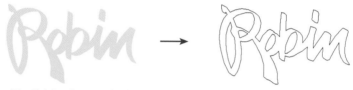

The Blob brush, set to the shape of a
calligraphic brush (page 78), and drawn
with a pressure-sensitive tablet.

In outline view, you can see
the art is one single shape.

I filled some of the blob shapes
with a blend; see pages 161–165.

TASK 14   Draw blobby shapes

Draw with the Blob brush as you would a real brush. Play with the brush for a few minutes, and then (on the opposite page) check the options you can set.

IMPORTANT NOTE: Make sure the *Stroke Color* box is **None,** otherwise the blob will draw with the Stroke Color, then switch that color to the Fill Color box, and you will go crazy trying to figure out what color it plans to use. So just always make sure the **stroke** is **None.**

1   Select the Blob brush, then drag to draw a funny shape.

2   Drag again, *using the same color,* and cross the first blob you did.

   If you look at the Outline view (from the View menu), you see the two blobs are actually one shape.

3   So now choose a different fill color (make sure the stroke color is None), then drag across the other blobs. Notice that the new strokes do *not* merge with Blob brush shapes that have different colors.

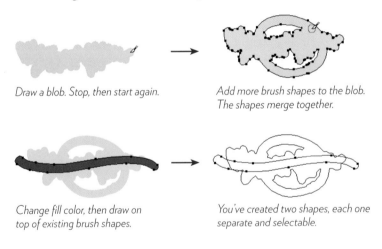

Draw a blob. Stop, then start again.

Add more brush shapes to the blob. The shapes merge together.

Change fill color, then draw on top of existing brush shapes.

You've created two shapes, each one separate and selectable.

TIP: To deselect a shape you just created, hold down the Command key (PC: Control key) and click in a blank spot. After you click, you still have the Blob brush.

TASK 15   Customize the Blob brush options

As with many of the drawing tools, much of the brush behavior is
determined in its options dialog box, so let's look at that.

1   Double-click the Blob brush tool in the Tools panel to open the
    "Blob brush Tool Options" dialog box, shown below.

2   Choose or adjust the following options:

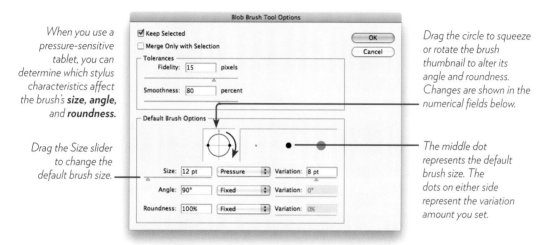

*When you use a
pressure-sensitive
tablet, you can
determine which stylus
characteristics affect
the brush's **size, angle,**
and **roundness.***

*Drag the Size slider
to change the
default brush size.*

*Drag the circle to squeeze
or rotate the brush
thumbnail to alter its
angle and roundness.
Changes are shown in the
numerical fields below.*

*The middle dot
represents the default
brush size. The
dots on either side
represent the variation
amount you set.*

Keep Selected: This option makes all shapes stay selected and you
can see their points, even as you add to them by drawing on top
(see the yellow example on the opposite page). This makes it easy
to see all parts of a merged path.

Merge Only with Selection: Blob shapes will merge only with
selected blob shapes of the same color. This includes the previous
shape if you've chosen the "Keep selected" option, or other blob
shapes *of the same color* that you manually select. This option
gives you more control of what gets merged into one shape.

Fidelity: This determines how far your mouse/stylus moves before
new anchor points are created. A higher value creates smoother, less
complex shapes.

Smoothness: Controls how much automatic smoothness is
applied to brush strokes. A higher number adds more smoothness,
but adds more distortion to the original shape.

Default Brush Options: These controls let you change the shape
of the brush and set a brush size, angle, and roundness.

TASK 16   Draw a blobby face

Select the Blob brush and draw a simple face, vaguely similar to the one below.

1   If you select the hair shape (below, center), you can see that it is merged with the face outline shape. The two shapes are merged because the Blob brush touched the face shape as you drew the hair. The eyes, nose, and mouth are *not* merged with the hair, or with each other, because they didn't touch each other as they were being drawn.

2   To make minor changes to the drawing, you can select a shape with the white Direct Selection tool, then drag anchor points around.

3   But for major changes, it's easier to erase part of the drawing and redraw it: Select the **Eraser tool** in the Tools panel, then drag across the parts of the drawing you want to revise (below, right).

4   Select the Blob brush again and draw the missing parts back in. *As long as the fill color is the same,* the new brush stroke shapes will merge with the existing shape.

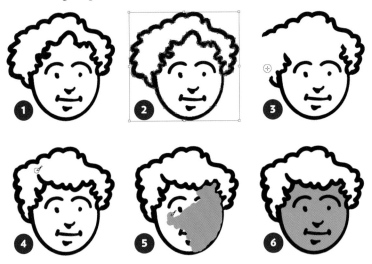

5   **To paint the inside of the face**, switch to "Draw Behind" mode: At the bottom of a single-column Tools panel, click the Drawing Mode icon, then choose "Draw Behind." At the bottom of a double-column Tools panel, click the "Draw Behind" icon.

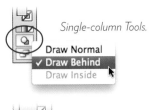

Single-column Tools.

Draw Normal
✓ Draw Behind
  Draw Inside

Select a color for the face, then use the Blob brush to paint the area. It *appears* as if you're covering up the other shapes!

Double-column Tools.

6   When you let go, the color snaps behind the black shapes. Make sure the black shapes overlap the color shape.

7   With the "Draw Behind" mode still selected, choose a light color and paint the whites of the eyes.

Aha—**the white went *all* the way behind, right?** While the eye shape is still selected, **bring it forward** until it's in the right place: Use the keyboard shortcut Command] (PC: Control]). That is, hold down the Command/Control key and tap the] key until the white of the eye is beneath the black pupil (to send it back, use the Command/Control key and the left bracket, [ ).

If you lost a shape under another shape, hold down the Command key (PC: Control key) and click where you know the object is hiding. Each time you Command/Control click, you reach down through another layer.

8   **Now paint inside the hair:** Make sure everything is *deselected,* and choose a fill color (stroke should still be None). You should still be in "Draw Behind" mode. If you brush into an inappropriate area accidentally, erase it with the Eraser tool.

9   Your artwork should now look similar to the example below, right. Each of the color shapes can still be selected independently, since separate colors aren't allowed to merge.

—continued

TIP: **Resize your brush on the fly:** Press the [to **reduce** the brush or] to **enlarge** the brush.

9 **Change the color of the face:** Use either the white or the black Selection tool to select the face color shape (below, left), then choose a color from the *Fill Color* pop-up panel in the Control panel.

The exact color you want to use is probably not in the pop-up Color panel. You can *create* a custom color (see Chapter 11). *Or* double-click on the color fill box in the Toolbar; this opens the Color Picker, from which you can choose a color (also see Chapter 11).

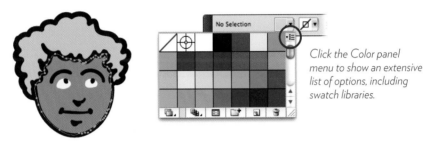

Click the Color panel menu to show an extensive list of options, including swatch libraries.

10 Remember, Blob brush shapes are selectable and editable, like any shape. You can move or scale entire shapes, and you can select individual anchor points to edit the shape. I used the black Selection tool, below, to reposition the pupils of the eyes.

TIP: You can merge Blob brush shapes with paths created by other tools. Just make sure the other artwork has no stroke, and choose exactly the same fill color for the Blob brush (the Eyedropper tool is handy for that; see Chapter 11).

TIP: Actually, you *can* put a stroke on a blob, if you like, *after* you draw it. Experiment with the brush for a while, using the following pages as a guide, and then try adding some of the brush effects you learned about on pages 79–82.

TASK 17   Try this!

A simple Blob brush technique I often use is shown below. Try it with any subject matter, such as an apple, a ball, or a pencil (yeah, good idea . . . a pencil!). The looseness that's achieved (and unavoidable) with this technique has an appeal that a more controlled drawing technique might not have. Let's title this painting *UFO Sighted Near Art Institute*.

1   Start by painting a black silhouette with the Blob brush. If you want to change the shape at any point, use the Eraser tool, erase the part that doesn't work, then redraw where necessary (see page 92, Steps 2 and 3). As long as you use the same fill color, the brush shapes will merge together.

2   Next, choose different fill colors and paint primitive shapes on top of the black. At any time you can select shapes to change their fill color, or delete shapes and re-paint them. These examples use flat colors to fill the shapes, but you can also use gradients (see Chapter 11).

The speed and simplicity of the Blob brush makes it one of my favorite drawing and painting tools.

Try this!

Create a poster of the alphabet in your language, each letter using a different brush technique (as well as other things you've learned in this book). Spend some time to explore the possibilities beyond the basics in this chapter— multiply effects, create crazy strokes, etc. Don't skip any letters—it is in the process of pushing yourself that you will go beyond the easy solutions and truly explore the possibilities. If you're in a class, share what you learned with your classmates. Even if your letterforms are not award-winning, you will learn so much about working in Illustrator in the process of creating them.

7 The Width Tool

The Width tool enables you to turn ordinary, single-weight paths into variable-width strokes. You can adjust the stroke width, slide the thick or thin part of a stroke along its path to reposition it, and you can create subtle or sudden changes in a stroke's width.

To summarize, it's easier than ever before to create flowing, variable width curves, and easier than ever to modify them.

Go wild with the Width tool

The following tasks introduce the Width tool basics that enable you to create almost *any* variable weight stroke. As you learn how to control stroke weights with the Width tool, try not to think about the advanced alien life forms that must be working as engineers at Adobe.

TASK 1   Modify a basic Pen tool stroke

1   Select the Pen tool and draw a simple curve with a minimal amount of anchor points. Our example has a 20-point stroke applied.

2   Select the Width tool in the Tools panel.

When the Width tool is over the path, a small diamond appears on the path. As you move the tool, the diamond moves along the path.

Press-and-drag outward from the stroke to widen it; this creates a width point at that spot.

3   The first time you create a width point on a path, it also creates width points and handles at both end points of the stroke; you won't *see* these end point width handles until you mouse over them.

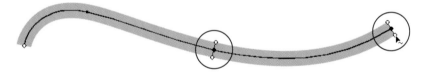

4   Again, slide the Width tool along the path, but this time, **double-click** where you want to add a width point, which opens the dialog box below.

Check the box to "Adjust Adjoining Width Points." This forces *that particular width point* to affect its adjacent width points, which helps smooth out the transitions between the thick and thin parts of the stroke. Click OK.

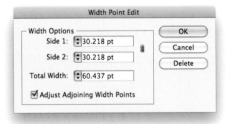

To open this dialog box at any time, double-click an existing width point, *or* double-click anywhere on a path (which also creates a new width point).

5   Press-and-drag a handle of the width control and drag *away* from the
    path to make the stroke wider.

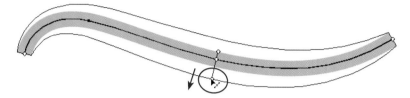

6   Move the Width tool over an end point and drag the width point
    handles *toward* the path to taper the stroke to a point. Repeat at the
    other end point.

7   Move the Width tool to another position on the path where you want
    to make the stroke thinner.

    Press-and-drag on the path to create another width point; drag the
    handles inward to make the stroke thinner.

8   Reposition a width point: Drag one of the width points along the path
    to see how it affects the stroke.

9   Make just one side of the path thicker or thinner: Option-drag
    (PC: Alt-drag) a width point handle.

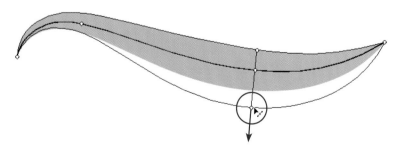

TASK 2   Create a variable width profile preset

After you use the Width tool to convert a uniform path into a variable width path, you may want to save the width profile as a preset that you can use again.

1   Select the Pen tool and draw several curved lines that could represent (hmmm) coffee steam (you don't need to bother drawing the cup). Notice that each path in the example has a minimal number of anchor points to keep the path simple and smooth.

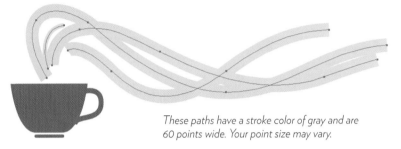

These paths have a stroke color of gray and are 60 points wide. Your point size may vary.

2   Select the Width tool, then press-and-drag a width point and handles out of the path to make the middle part of the stroke wider.

Move the Width tool to one of the end points; press-and-drag the handles in toward the path to create a pointy end. Repeat for the other end point.

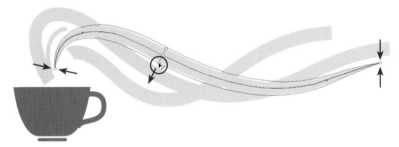

3   With the modified path selected, open the *Variable Width Profile* menu of presets, located in the Control panel (shown below).

Click the "Add to Profiles" icon in the pop-up panel's bottom-left corner. In the "Variable Width Profile" dialog box that opens, name the profile "Coffee steam," then click OK.

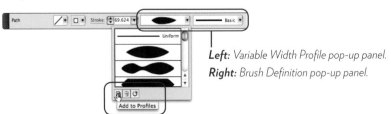

Left: *Variable Width Profile pop-up panel.*
Right: *Brush Definition pop-up panel.*

4 Select the remaining steam paths (hold down the Shift key to select multiple objects), then go back to the *Variable Width Profile* pop-up menu and choose the "Coffee steam" profile from the list.

The remaining steam paths are converted to the custom width profile.

5 **Now try this:** Select all of the steam paths, then open the "Transparency" panel (Window > Transparency).

Click the "Blending Mode" pop-up menu and choose "Multiply." Also experiment with the other blending modes. These different modes can dramatically affect how colors and shades of different objects interact with each other.

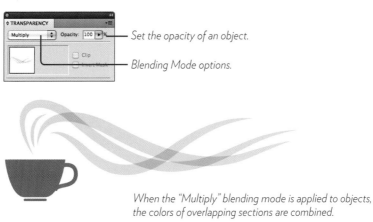

Set the opacity of an object.

Blending Mode options.

When the "Multiply" blending mode is applied to objects, the colors of overlapping sections are combined.

6 **Also try this:** Select all of the steam paths. From the *Brush Definition* pop-up panel in the Control panel (shown at the bottom of the opposite page), choose "Chalk – Scribble." Select each path individually, then use the Transparency panel to assign varying "Opacity" values (shown above).

TASK 3 Create a discontinuous width point

Most width points create a gradual transition between width settings on a path and are called *continuous* width points. Occasionally you might want to create a stroke that has an instant change in width. In this case you need to create a *discontinuous* width point.

1 Use the Pen tool to draw a simple path similar to the one shown below, left.

2 Select the Width tool, position the tool over the hump section of the path, then press-and-drag outward, away from the path, to make the stroke wider (below, right).

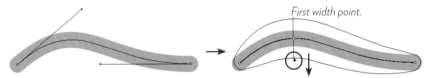

First width point.

3 Position the Width tool near the right end point, then press-and-drag on the path, but drag inward, toward the path, to make the stroke thinner (below, left).

Drag the second width point to the left. You can see the transition between the two width points becomes less gradual (below, right).

Second width point.

These shapes were drawn as a 1-point stroke with the Pencil tool, modified with the Width tool, and assigned a blend mode of Overlay.

4 Keep dragging the width point to the left until it's *on top* of the first width point (below, left). This intersection of two stroke widths is called a *discontinuous* width point.

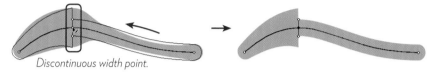

Discontinuous width point.

5 **Now try this:** Drag the second width point back to the right side, *almost* all the way to the end point on the right. Then drag the first width point to the right, near the second width point. How close you get determines the shape of the path.

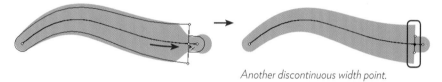

Another discontinuous width point.

Try this!

This project will give you great practice using the Pen tool to create smooth lines, and then using the Width tool to make elegant shapes of those lines. If you don't feel confident enough yet to draw these curves by eye, scan this image and use the tracing-layer technique we explained on pages 67–69.

Above:
This outline view shows the uniform paths drawn with the Pen tool, based on a scanned sketch.

Below:
Preview mode shows the paths modified with the Width tool.

I drew the swan's face with the Pen tool, then filled it with color.

8 Draw with Live Trace

Illustrator can trace raster images, such as digital photos or scans of drawn or sketched images. It has two kinds of tracing: manual and automatic. Pages 67–74 showed how you can *manually* trace a reference file using drawing tools, but Illustrator's Live Trace feature creates the tracing for you *automatically*.

Automatic tracing is different from the manual version in several ways.

ONE: *It's extremely fast.* And after you trace an image, the finished drawing is editable, just like any other artwork in Illustrator.

TWO: *It's extremely accurate,* depending on the tracing options you choose.

THREE: *It's extremely flexible.* You can create vastly different drawings from the same source file.

FOUR: *It's extremely easy.* Choose from tracing presets to make complex or simple tracings.

FIVE: Did we mention *fast?*

Live Trace presets and settings

The easiest and quickest way to trace an image is to choose a preset. Experiment with all the presets so you'll have a good idea of what each one does.

TASK 1   Trace an image using presets

1   You're going to place an image on the page. For now, choose a photograph about 5 x 7 inches, 72 ppi (pixels per inch). You can experiment later with higher resolutions and larger images (Illustrator is fast, but there's no point in slowing it down while exploring different settings).

Choose File > Place…, then locate a photo to trace (below, left).

2   With the black Selection tool, click on the image to select it. The Control panel, shown below, displays some general information about the image and a few options (Embed, Edit Original, Live Trace).

3   Click the *Tracing presets and options* button, circled below. For now, choose "Color 6" from that menu. The tracing appears a second or two later. Wow.

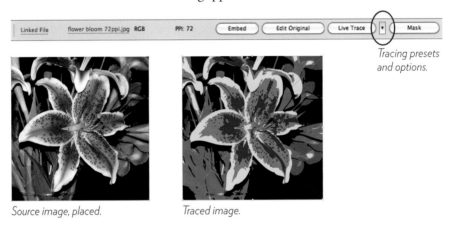

Tracing presets and options.

Source image, placed.   *Traced image.*

4   After an image is traced (and still selected), the Control panel changes to show options specific to the preset you used. You can change these at this point, and the new options will affect the selected image.

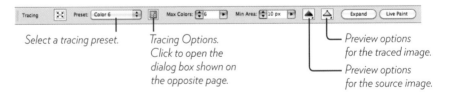

Select a tracing preset.   *Tracing Options. Click to open the dialog box shown on the opposite page.*   *Preview options for the traced image.*   *Preview options for the source image.*

You can also open the "Tracing Options" dialog box to tweak the selected tracing (opposite page). **And be sure to read Task 4 for more options!**

TASK 2   Customize the tracing settings

In the "Tracing Options" dialog box, as explained below, you can modify the settings, preview the results, and save the modified preset to use again. Make sure the tracing is *selected* if you want these options to apply.

1   To open the "Tracing Options" dialog box, click the *Tracing Options* icon in the Control panel (shown at the bottom of the opposite page).

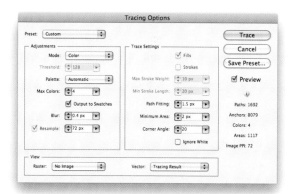

TIP: You can also get this dialog box *before* you make the tracing in the first place: In the *Tracing presets and options* menu (Task 1.3), choose "Tracing Options...."

2   If your placed image is *selected,* click the "Preview" checkbox to see the results as you change settings.

Try these settings in the "Adjustments" section:

Change "Max Colors" to 4 to limit the colors used even further.

Check the "Output to Swatches" box. The colors created by the "Max Colors" option will be added to the Swatches panel.

Try these settings in the "Trace Settings" section:

Select "Ignore White" if you want the white parts to be transparent instead of opaque white, such as when you trace a scan of a sketch drawn on white paper (see the following page).

Change these settings only if you don't like the preview results of a tracing: The "Path Fitting," "Minimum Area," and "Corner Angle" settings determine how much accuracy and detail is preserved.

3   When you're satisfied with the preview results, click "Trace" and *the image is retraced and replaced.*

4   If you'd like **to use these settings again,** click "Save Preset...." In the "Save Tracing Preset" dialog box that opens, name the preset, then click OK. The custom preset will now appear in the preset menus, both in the Control panel and in the "Tracing Options" dialog box.

Trace your way to great art

Follow these easy steps to learn several ways to take advantage of Live Trace.

TASK 3   Trace a sketch

For printed pieces, I often trace my sketches to use in the printed product, rather than printing the scanned, raster version of the file. Vector files (the traced ones) are very small compared to raster (pixel-based, scanned) files. Best of all, the tracing can be enlarged or reduced without any quality degradation.

1   Place a scan of a sketch: Choose File > Place…. It appears on the page with an X through it because it's a linked file—that's okay.

   If you don't have a sketch, scribble on a piece of paper and scan that.

   Or, as we have often done, take a photo of the piece of paper and place that photo.

Scanned from John's sketchbook: a stranger across the aisle on an overseas flight.

2 Choose Object > Live Trace > Tracing Options....

If a warning tells you the tracing might be slow because the file is large, don't worry, you can resample it to a lower resolution in the next step.

3 In the "Tracing Options" dialog box, I adjusted the following settings for this specific image:

A higher **Threshold** *prevents weak lines from disappearing.*
I checked both **Fills** *and* **Strokes** *for more accurate tracing on this drawing.*
I set a small **Minimum Area** *so it would pick up the tiny lines of the sketch.*
A bit of **Blur** *often helps make the traced lines smoother.*
I **resampled** *the resolution down to 150 pixels so the file wouldn't be so large.*
I chose to **Ignore White** *to avoid creating opaque, white-filled paths. This means the tracing will be transparent so objects behind it will be visible, as the page number on the opposite page.*

4 Click "Trace."

The tracing might happen so fast and look so much like the original that you're not sure if anything actually happened.

Click the *Vector result* preview button in the Control panel (circled below). If "Tracing Result" is selected, the tracing is what you see. The tracing has an X running through it, as seen on page 106.

From the *Vector result* menu, you can also choose "Outlines" to see the paths that have been created.

The tracing is now a *tracing object*. To convert it into *paths* (as shown in red, below, right,) or a *Live Paint group,* see the following page.

TASK 4 Expand a tracing object

The *tracing object* is made up of the source image *and* the vector art tracing. **To work with the tracing as you can with any other vector art,** you must **expand** the tracing object, which separates the vector paths from the source image so you can work with the paths.

Keep in mind that once you expand a tracing object, you can no longer change the tracing options.

1 With a tracing object selected, click the "Expand" button in the Control panel.

Or choose Object > Live Trace > Expand.

2 Now you can see and work with the paths.

Press Command Y (PC: Control Y) to view the Outline mode; press the keyboard shortcut again to return to Preview mode (or use the View menu).

Press Command H (PC: Control H) to hide the path points, but still keep the object selected.

Remember (from Chapter 3), use the *black* Selection tool to select the entire object, and use the *white* Direct Selection tool to select individual paths.

Convert a tracing object to a Live Paint group

Live Paint is a powerful painting technique that enables you to assign colors to the faces and edges (fills and strokes) of shapes in more versatile ways than with any other feature in Illustrator. Learn about Live Paint in Chapter 14.

Live Paint

• With a tracing object selected, click the "Live Paint" button in the Control panel.

Or choose Object > Live Paint > Convert to Live Paint.

Delete a tracing object

To delete a tracing but keep the placed source image, select the tracing object, then choose Object > Live Trace > Release.

TIP: To create a tracing object and convert it to paths in one step, choose Object > Live Trace > Make and Expand.

Other reasons to love Live Trace

We've just scratched the surface, but you'll find lots of other ways to use Live Trace in your projects. We've traced scans of traditional paintings and also digital raster paintings created at a small size, then enlarged the vector tracing up to thirty or forty inches wide to output on stretched canvas.

The image traced, shown as path outlines.

The image, traced.

We've also sketched rough handlettering on paper, scanned and traced it, then expanded it and cleaned it up with the selection tools, Eraser tool, and sometimes the Blob brush.

In the example below, I handlettered the logo, cleaned it up as much as possible in Photoshop, then use Live Trace to create a vector version that I can enlarge to any size.

This is the vector tracing of a hand-lettered logo.

The logo's editable vector paths are shown in outline mode.

Try this!

Use the Tasks in this chapter to experiment with creating a tracing object. Use a photo that you like and turn it into an art piece. Scan your signature and create a digital version of it. Trace old images from out-of-copyright books to use in your design work. Expand the tracing object and color the fills and strokes, or reshape the paths. Even if you don't have an immediate use for this tool, you want to embed the idea into your fingers and brain so when the perfect project for tracing appears, you are ready with the tool.

I scanned this image from a sixteenth-century book.

I cleaned up the image in Photoshop to make it easier to work with in Illustrator.

I did a Live Trace in Illustrator, previewing the Tracing Options until I got what I wanted, then cleaned it up some more, then roughened it up a bit (Effect > Distort & Transform > Roughen) because the organic lines are so interesting.

Section 3
More Essentials

"If you think you've stopped learning, you're going to get lapped." *Robby Gordon, race car driver*

Everything you've learned so far is important for a basic understanding of Illustrator, its tools, and the concept of vector drawing or painting.

In this section you'll learn about layers, how to work with type, and how to use and manage color in many ways: create color groups, custom swatches panels, global colors, gradients, and more.

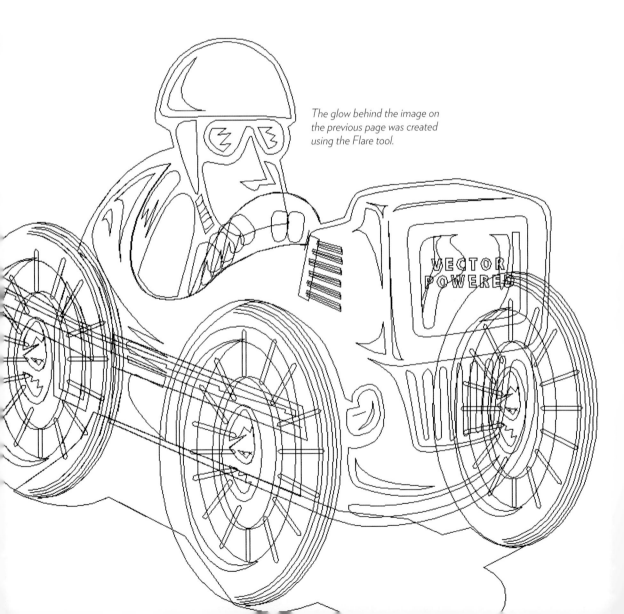

The glow behind the image on the previous page was created using the Flare tool.

9 Working with Layers

Every Illustrator document is created with one layer, or level, on which to create art, and or many projects, that's all you need. But for a lot of work, multiple layers are a necessity and a lifesaver—or at least a project-saver.

As you create artwork, Illustrator puts each shape and path on its own layer or sublayer. You can manually create new layers and arrange their stacking arrangement in whatever order you need. Layers give you the ability to keep complex (or simple) artwork organized, and make it easy to manage, select, and modify the various items in a project.

Layers can also be used to create variations of artwork, or specific elements of the artwork, then can be hidden or revealed to preview different versions of a project.

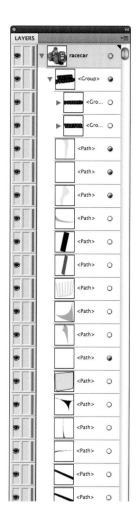

The Layers panel

The Layers panel shows every shape, path, guide, and piece of text that's included in your artwork so you can manage, select, and modify any object separately and easily.

The characteristics of the Layers panel

You can drag layers to change the stacking order, turn a layer's visibility on or off, lock layers so they can't be changed or selected accidently, and much more.

Inspect the Layers panel below and its callouts on the following page for an overview of the visual clues that this panel provides, then use Task 2 as practice for becoming comfortable with layers.

TASK 1   Customize the appearance of the Layers panel

1   Open the Layers panel: Choose Window > Layers.

2   Open the Layers panel menu (in the top-right corner of the panel), and choose "Panel Options…."

3   In the "Layers Panel Options" dialog box that opens, set a size in the "Row Size" section. I chose "Other" and entered a value of 75 pixels so I can see everything clearly.

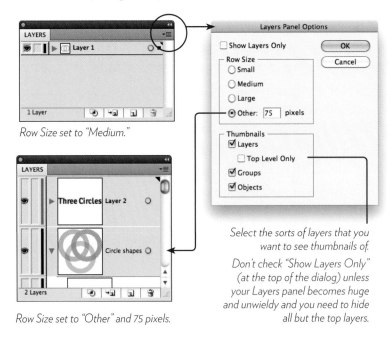

Row Size set to "Medium."

Row Size set to "Other" and 75 pixels.

Select the sorts of layers that you want to see thumbnails of.

Don't check "Show Layers Only" (at the top of the dialog) unless your Layers panel becomes huge and unwieldy and you need to hide all but the top layers.

The Layers panel below contains the layers for the "Three Circles" art and text, shown on the right. Notice that the purple path is selected and its layer (below) displays a small, square *selection icon* in the selection column of the Layers panel. Notice also that one blue horizontal guide is visible on the right, although there are two Guide layers in the Layers panel; that's because I clicked the eyeball icon in the visibility column of the other Guide layer to hide its content.

Three Circles

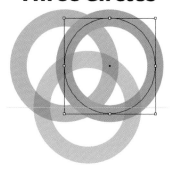

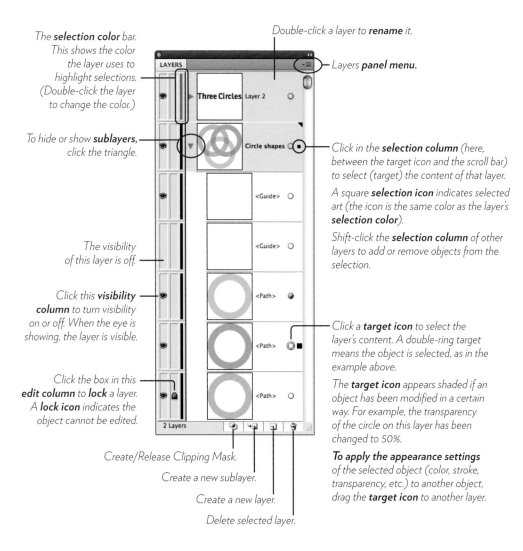

The **selection color** bar. This shows the color the layer uses to highlight selections. (Double-click the layer to change the color.)

To hide or show **sublayers**, click the triangle.

The visibility of this layer is off.

Click this **visibility column** to turn visibility on or off. When the eye is showing, the layer is visible.

Click the box in this **edit column** to **lock** a layer. A **lock icon** indicates the object cannot be edited.

Double-click a layer to **rename** it.

Layers **panel menu.**

Click in the **selection column** (here, between the target icon and the scroll bar) to select (target) the content of that layer.

A square **selection icon** indicates selected art (the icon is the same color as the layer's **selection color**).

Shift-click the **selection column** of other layers to add or remove objects from the selection.

Click a **target icon** to select the layer's content. A double-ring target means the object is selected, as in the example above.

The **target icon** appears shaded if an object has been modified in a certain way. For example, the transparency of the circle on this layer has been changed to 50%.

To apply the appearance settings of the selected object (color, stroke, transparency, etc.) to another object, drag the **target icon** to another layer.

Create/Release Clipping Mask.

Create a new sublayer.

Create a new layer.

Delete selected layer.

117

Manage a document with multiple layers

This is an example of how you might work with layers in a project. Walk through this task to become familiar with the process because you will use it often.

TASK 2 Manage a document with multiple layers

1 Create a new document.

2 Draw an ellipse: Select the Ellipse tool, then drag to draw an ellipse. To constrain the ellipse to a perfect circle, hold down the Shift key as you drag.

3 Adjust the object's appearance: In the Control panel, set the *Stroke Weight* to 40 points; choose a color swatch from the *Stroke Color* pop-up menu; set a *Color Fill* of None.

4 Duplicate the circle: With the black Selection tool, hold down the Option key (PC: Alt key) and drag the circle to the right; also hold down the Shift key to constrain the movement to a perfectly horizontal path. The result of the drag is shown below, right.

 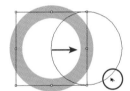 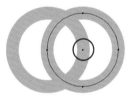

A circle with a 40-point color stroke applied. | *As you drag, the pointer icon (circled) indicates a duplicate will be created.* | *The duplicate circle in its position.*

5 With the black Selection tool, select the duplicate circle. From the Control panel, choose a different color (below, left).

6 Make another circle: With the black Selection tool, hold down the Option key (PC: Alt key) and drag a circle to the position shown below (center).

7 Assign a different stroke color to the newest circle (below, right).

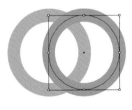 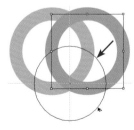 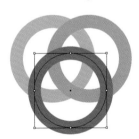

Assign a new stroke color. | *Duplicate a circle in this position.* | *Assign a new stroke color.*

8   **Open the Layers panel:** Choose Window > Layers.

9   **Rename the layer:** Double-click the layer, then in the "Layer Options" dialog box, type "Circle shapes" in the "Name" field.

10 **Show the sublayers:** Click the disclosure triangle on the left side of the layer thumbnail to reveal three sublayers, one for each shape.

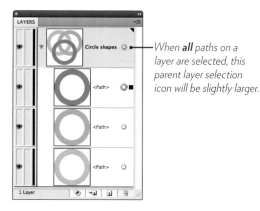

Click the triangle to show the sublayers (shown to the right).

*When **all** paths on a layer are selected, this parent layer selection icon will be slightly larger.*

11 **Select different objects:** Click the *target icon* (the tiny circle on the right) of different sublayers. This is an alternative way to select paths when the artwork is too complex to easily make a selection by clicking directly on the artwork.

12 **Hide or show layers:** Click the visibility icon next to different layers to hide the layer content of the artwork. Click the icon again to show the object.

13 **Lock layers:** Click the edit column next to a layer to place a lock icon in it. This is most useful when you're drawing on top of other paths and don't want to accidently select or modify underlying objects.

14 **Move layers and see the effects:** Select a layer and drag it up or down in the stacking order. The arrangement of layers makes a big difference in the appearance of the artwork—try it.

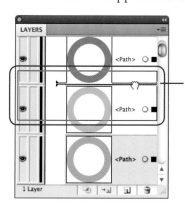

When you drag a layer up or down in the stacking order, a black bar appears when the pointer (the hand icon) is positioned over the drop zone between layers.

Let go when the bar is positioned where you want the new layer to move.

A few other features of layers

There are a number of ways to do several common actions. Experiment with these options so they will be familiar to you when you need them.

TASK 3   Create a new parent layer

When you create a new, blank, parent layer, it is always placed *just above the currently selected layer,* so first select the existing layer appropriately.

- Click the *Create New Layer* button at the bottom of the Layers panel.
- *Or* open the Layers panel menu (from the top-right corner of the Layers panel), then choose "New Layer…."

TASK 4   Create a sublayer for a parent layer

- Select the parent layer, then click the *Create New Sublayer* button at the bottom of the Layers panel.
- *Or* select the parent layer, open the Layers panel menu, then choose "New Sublayer…."

TASK 5   Duplicate an existing layer

- Drag a layer on top of the *Create New Layer* button at the bottom of the Layers panel.
- *Or* select a layer, then from the Layers panel menu, choose "Duplicate *'name of layer.'*"
- *Or* hold down the Option key (PC: Alt key) as you drag a layer to another position in the stacking order.

TASK 6   Delete a layer

- Select one (or more) layers, then click the Trash icon in the bottom-right corner of the Layers panel.
- Select one (or more) layers, then drag the layers to the Trash.
- Select one (or more) layers, then from the Layers panel menu, choose "Delete Selection."

TASK 7   Collect the art on individual layers into one layer

You can select various *parent* layers or a group of *sublayers* from the same parent and combine them into one collection, which creates a new parent layer with sublayers.

1 Hold down the Command key (PC: Control key) and select the layers that contain artwork you want to collect into one layer.

2 From the Layers panel menu, choose "Collect in New Layer."

10 Working with Type

There are many reasons to set type in Illustrator—to create a graphic, a logo, brochures, flyers, business cards, letterhead, rack cards, posters. Illustrator's type tools provide all of the options and control you need, no matter what your project's typographic ambitions may be.

In this chapter, you'll learn the basics of typesetting in Illustrator, how to create styles with multiple attributes, how to use tabs and indents, and more.

If you're an experienced InDesign user (or if you've read the type section of *The Non-Designer's InDesign Book*), you'll find Illustrator's type features very familiar.

Basic typesetting

Methods for importing existing text

There are several ways to get type into your document:

- Copy text from another document and paste it into an Illustrator document. Pasted text does *not* retain its formatting.

- Import text: Choose File > Place. Select a text file to import, then click "Place." Imported text retains character and paragraph formatting, a nice advantage when there's lots of text and it's already been formatted.

Methods for creating type within Illustrator

Illustrator provides four basic ways to create type, outlined below and explained in detail on the following pages. Once you've created the type you need, you're almost unlimited in what you can do with it.

- **Point type:** Point type is when you set a point and type. With the Type tool, click in the document and type. The type path extends as you type.

THE GOLDEN SPEECH

- **Paragraph type in a text frame:** Choose the Type tool, drag diagonally to create a text boundary, then type inside of it. When the text reaches a boundary edge, it wraps to fit the shape (below, left).

- **Paragraph type in a shape or area:** Draw a shape, use the Area Type tool to click the shape's path, then type to fill the shape (below, right).

- **Type on a path:** Type is set to follow the edge of an open or closed path (a line or shape).

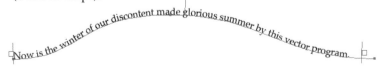

TASK 1   Create point type

1   Choose the Type tool.

2   Click in a document, then start typing. The text extends to the *right,*
    so make sure you click on the *left* side of your document. It continues
    to the right until you hit Return/Enter or stop typing.

The placement of the small dot on the baseline (circled above)
indicates the **type alignment:** left, right, or centered.

3   **Resize the type.** Do one of the following:

    • With the black Selection tool, click on the text to select it.
      Hold down the Shift key (to resize the type proportionally), and
      drag one of the corner handles of the text frame diagonally upward.

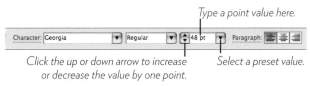

    • *Or* use the *Font Size* pop-up menu in the Control panel.

Type a point value here.

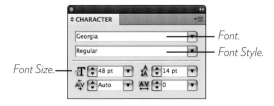

Click the up or down arrow to increase   *Select a preset value.*
or decrease the value by one point.

    • Open the Character panel, then set a point size in the *Font Size*
      pop-up menu, shown below.

4   **Change the font:** Use the *Font* pop-up menu in the Control panel or in
    the Character panel to choose another font.

Font Size. ── [Character panel] ── *Font.*
Font Style.

TIP: To start another piece of
point type, you have to "let go"
of the first one: Hold down the
Command key (PC: Control key)
and click in an empty spot.

5   **Change the font style:** Use the *Font Style* pop-up menu in the Control
    panel or the Character panel to change to italic, bold, etc. (if that font
    family includes different styles).

TASK 2 Create paragraph type in a text frame

1 Choose the Type tool.

2 Drag diagonally to create a rectangular shape in which the text will be restrained.

3 **Type some text.** When the text reaches the boundary of the text frame, it automatically wraps to the next line (so don't hit a Return/Enter).

In port. 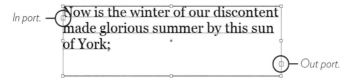 *Out port.*

A paragraph text frame has an **in port** and an **out port** (circled above). The ports indicate if there's more text linked to the text frame.

> **Empty ports** mean all text is visible.
>
> An out port with a **red plus sign** (below, left) means the box contains overflow text that's not visible. In this case, you must enlarge the existing text frame, or *link* it to another text frame so the extra text flows into it (see the following page).
>
> A port with a **blue triangle** in it indicates that *linked* text is coming into, or flowing out of, the current text frame (below, right).

Now is the winter of our discontent
Made glorious summer by this sun of
York; and all the clouds that lour'd
upon our house in the deep bosom of
the ocean buried. Now are our brows
bound with victorious wreaths; our

Now is the winter of our discontent
Made glorious summer by this sun of
York; and all the clouds that lour'd
upon our house in the deep bosom of
the ocean buried. Now are our brows
bound with victorious wreaths; our

4 **Paste text into the text frame:** Copy some lengthy text from a document or a web page, then paste it into the box you created in Step 2.

5 **Resize the text frame:** With the black Selection tool, drag the right handle of the text frame to the right to enlarge the box and lengthen the lines, *or* drag the bottom-middle handle to make the box deeper.

Now is the winter of our discontent
Made glorious summer by this sun of York; and all the
clouds that lour'd upon our house in the deep bosom of
the ocean buried. Now are our brows bound with victorious wreaths; our bruised arms hung up for monu-
ments; our stern alarums chang'd to merry meetings,

6   **Reshape a text frame:** Select the white Direct Selection tool, then marquee around a corner point of the text frame to select it.

Drag the corner point to a new position. Hold down the Shift key as you drag to constrain the drag to a horizontal path (below, left).

Mr. Speaker, We have heard your declaration and perceive your care of our estate. I do assure you there is no prince that loves his subjects better, or whose love can countervail our love. There is no jewel, be it of never so rich a price, which I set before this jewel: I mean your love. For I do esteem it more than any treasure or riches; for that we know how to prize, but love and thanks I count invaluable. And, though God hath

Mr. Speaker, We have heard your declaration and perceive your care of our estate. I do assure you there is no prince that loves his subjects better, or whose love can countervail our love. There is no jewel, be it of never so rich a price, which I set before this jewel: I mean your love. For I do esteem it more than any treasure or riches; for that we know how to prize, but love and thanks I count invalu-

Drag a corner point to reshape a text frame.

Add two anchor points (circled), then drag the anchor point between to a new position.

Add points to the text frame (above, right) for more reshaping: Select the Pen tool and hover over the text frame path. When the Pen tool pointer icon changes to show a plus sign next to it, click to add an anchor point. Add additional anchor points along the path as needed. Get the white Direct Selection tool and drag those anchor points to positions to create the shape you want.

7   **Link overflow text to another text frame:** With the black Selection tool, click the overflow *out port* of a text frame (circled below, middle).

The pointer changes appearance (below, right) to indicate that it's *loaded* with the overflow text.

Drag the loaded pointer diagonally to create another text frame. When you let go, the hidden text flows into the linked text frame.

Two linked text frames. On the right, the loaded text pointer is ready to drag a third text frame so more text can flow into it.

Drag diagonally with the loaded pointer to create a linked text frame.

Mr. Speaker, We have heard your declaration and perceive your care of our estate. I do assure you there is no prince that loves his subjects better, or whose love can countervail our love. There is no jewel, be it of never so rich a price, which I set before this jewel: I mean your love. For I do esteem it more than any treasure or riches; for that we know how to prize, but love and thanks I count

invaluable. And, though God hath raised me high, yet this I count the glory of my Crown, that I have reigned with your loves. This makes me that I do not so much rejoice that God hath made me to be a Queen, as to be a Queen over so thankful a people. Therefore I have cause to wish nothing more than to content the subject and that is a duty which I owe. Neither do I desire to live

To load the pointer with overflow text *(shown above), click this out port.*

*Linked text frames are visually linked with **blue text threads.** To hide the text threads, choose View > Hide Text Threads.*

TASK 3   Create text in a shape

1   Select the Ellipse tool, then drag diagonally to draw an ellipse.

Hold down the Shift key as you drag to constrain the ellipse
to a perfect circle.

It doesn't matter if the shape has a color fill or stroke; the Area Type
tool removes any such attributes in Step 3.

2   Select the Area Type tool (it's hidden under the Type tool).

3   Click anywhere on the circle's *path* (make sure you click the *path*
and not inside the shape).

4   Type text, paste text from another document, or import text into the
circle (choose File > Place to import).

As with text in a text frame (pages 124–125), overflow text is indicated
by an out port with a red plus sign in it (shown below).

5   Set a text inset margin: Choose Type > Area Type Options....

In the "Offset" section, set the "Inset Spacing" value to 12 pt.

Click the "Preview" checkbox to see the results (below, right) and
change the settings if desired.

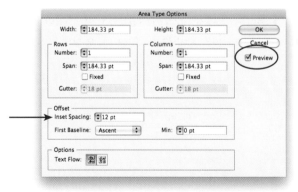

Notice that you can also
set **rows and columns**
within the text area.
Experiment with this!

TIP: You can also use this dialog box to
set an inset (or rows and/or columns)
in a regular paragraph type text frame.

TASK 4 Create type on a closed path

1   Select the Ellipse tool, then drag diagonally to draw an ellipse.
    If you want a perfect circle, hold down the Shift key as you drag.

    It doesn't matter if the shape has a color fill or stroke; the Type-on-a-Path tool removes any such attributes in Step 3.

2   Select the Type-on-a-Path tool.

3   Click the top-center edge of the *path* (that is, not inside the shape).

4   **Type** a few clever words on the path.

5   Choose the white Direct Selection tool.

    Three brackets appear on the path: a center bracket and end brackets on both sides of the type. Drag these brackets to position the type on the path where you want.

    To drag a bracket, hover the white Direct Selection tool over a bracket until a small *bracket icon* appears next to the pointer (shown below); drag the bracket to slide the type left or right along the path.

    To help prevent the type from flipping to the other side of the path, hold down the Command key (PC: Control key) as you drag.

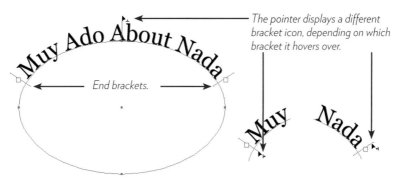

End brackets.

The pointer displays a different bracket icon, depending on which bracket it hovers over.

6   **Apply effects to type on a path:** Double-click the Type-on-a-Path tool icon in the Tools panel to open the "Type on a Path Options" dialog box.

    With the text path selected, choose different options in the "Effect" pop-up menu. Also experiment with the other options.

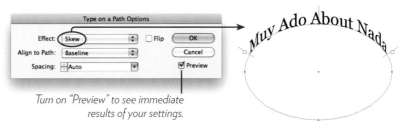

Turn on "Preview" to see immediate results of your settings.

TASK 5   Create type on an open path

1   Select a drawing tool (the Pencil, Pen, or Paintbrush tool) and draw a path similar to the one below.

2   Select the Type-on-a-Path tool (it's hidden under the Type tool), then click the left side of the path.

3   Type some clever words on the path.

Muy Ado About Nada

If the type is too large to fit on the path, **adjust the font size:** With the Type tool, triple-click the text to select it. Go to the *Font Size* pop-up menu in the Control menu and choose a smaller font size.

4   **To reposition the type on the path,** choose the white Direct Selection tool. Hover over the left end bracket until the small bracket icon appears, then drag the bracket to the right.

Muy Ado About Nada   *Muy Ado About Nada*

Drag the end bracket to the right to move the type to the right.

5   Position the type where you want it, then enlarge the text (below) so that it fills the path.

6   **Adjust the path's curve:** Choose the white Direct Selection tool. Click on the curve, then drag anchor points, direction handles, or path segments to reshape the curved path.

Muy Ado About Nada
SANTA FE *Shakespeare* SOCIETY

The Character panel

The character formatting options found in the Control panel are convenient for basic formatting, but you often need more than basics. The Character panel contains a complete set of options for typographic control at the *character* level (meaning the controls apply to individual characters that are *selected,* as opposed to the *paragraph* level where options apply to the entire paragraph).

To open the Character panel, choose Window > Type > Character. *Or* click the word "Character" in the Control panel, circled below.

TASK 6   Format text with the Character panel menu

The Character panel menu contains a pop-up menu of options.

If you don't see all the ——— Panel menu.
options shown here,
click this double-arrow
cycle button to cycle
through the panel
options.

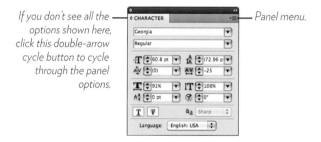

1   Choose the Type tool, and set this line of text: **To Town To Vote.**

2   Choose the black Selection tool, which automatically selects the text.

To Town To Vote

3   Open the Character panel menu. Choose the font named Georgia, and a font size of 60 point.

4   From the Character panel menu, choose "All Caps." The *selected* type is converted to all caps formatting.

TO TOWN TO VOTE

5   Now choose "Small Caps," and you see that the *selected* type is converted to small caps formatting.

TO TOWN TO VOTE

—continued

6 You can see a common typographic problem in Steps 2 and 5: There is too much letterspacing between the T and the o, due to the shape of the T and all that open space under its crossbar. The same spacing problem happens with the V and the o, as shown below, left. You need to adjust the spacing between the letter pairs. Adobe calls it *kerning* when you adjust the space between *two* characters, and *tracking* when you adjust the space between a *range* of characters.

To adjust the letterspacing in the entire line automatically: With the black Selection tool, click on the line of type to select it; in the Character panel, change the kerning value (see the callout in the panel below) from "Auto" to "Optical." The result is shown below, right.

T₁o V₁ote   To Town To Vote

Too much space.   *Extra space automatically removed.*

7 **Adjust the letterspacing manually:** With the Type tool, click between a T and o.

Click the up or down arrow on the left side of the *kerning* field to change the value; watch the characters shift. Hold down the Shift key as you click to change 5 times the value with each click.

The increment in which the value changes is based on the setting in the Preferences' (see page 6) Type pane; the default "Tracking" value is 20. We suggest you change that to 5 so you have more precise control.

8 Because kerning and tracking are so intrinsic to working with type, we suggest you learn the keyboard shortcuts:

Mac: Option Left *or* RightArrow for small increments;
　　 Option Command Left *or* RightArrow for 5 times the increment.

PC:　 Alt Left or RightArrow for small increments;
　　 Alt Control Left-or-RightArrow for 5 times the increment.

9 Experiment with the other settings in the Character panel. Use the tool tips to see what each field controls.

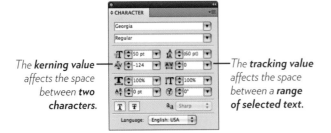

*The **kerning value** affects the space between **two** characters.*

*The **tracking value** affects the space between a **range** of selected text.*

TIP: If you're using one of the Selection tools, you can double-click in the text to **switch to the Type tool.**

The Paragraph panel

The paragraph level formatting options in the Control panel are convenient, but limited. For a full set of options, open the Paragraph panel: Window > Type > Paragraph. *Or* click the word "Paragraph" in the Control panel, shown circled below.

TASK 7   Change paragraph formatting

1   Create a paragraph of type, as you did on page 124.

2   **To apply paragraph formatting to all the paragraphs in the text frame:** With the black Selection tool, select the text frame, then experiment with the various options in the Paragraph panel (shown below).

3   **To apply paragraph formatting to one specific paragraph:** With the Text tool, click anywhere within a paragraph, then experiment with different settings in the Paragraph panel.

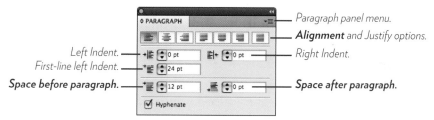

Left Indent.
First-line left Indent.
Space before paragraph.

Paragraph panel menu.
Alignment *and Justify options.*
Right Indent.
Space after paragraph.

Click the up or down arrows to change the values in 1-point increments.

Hold down the Shift key as you click to change the values in 6-point increments.

You can also type numbers into the value fields.

TASK 8   Create hanging punctuation

Hanging punctuation moves punctuation marks outside the paragraph margins to make edges look more even (and more professional).

1   With the Type tool, click in a paragraph that uses an opening quotation mark.

2   From the Paragraph panel menu, choose "Roman Hanging Punctuation."

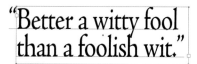

Before hanging punctuation is applied.   *After hanging punctuation is applied.*

131

The Glyphs panel

Many fonts have alternate characters built into them, such as swash versions, ornaments, oldstyle figures, fractions, foreign alphabets, etc. The Glyphs panel is the best way to access these alternative characters. It lets you view *glyphs* (characters of any sort) and insert them into your document.

OpenType fonts usually offer more glyphs to choose from. Font formats other than OpenType (TrueType or Postscript) may or may not have alternate characters included. Check the Glyph panel to find out.

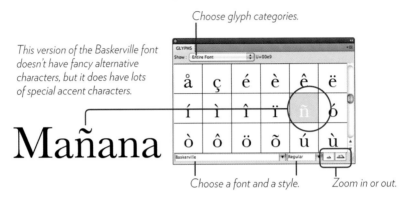

Choose glyph categories.

This version of the Baskerville font doesn't have fancy alternative characters, but it does have lots of special accent characters.

Choose a font and a style.

Zoom in or out.

TASK 9 Insert glyphs into text

1 Open the Glyphs panel: Choose Type > Glyphs. The panel shows all the characters available in the currently selected font.

2 **Replace a character with an alternate character:** Use the Type tool to select a character (or a pair of characters such as ff) that you want to replace with an alternate character or a ligature (a specially designed combination of two characters).

3 Double-click a glyph in the panel to replace the selected character/s.

4 **Insert a glyph:** With the Type tool, click in the text at the position you want to insert a glyph (perhaps an ornament or fraction); double-click the glyph in the panel.

Bickham Script with regular characters.

Bickham Script using several alternate characters. This gorgeous font has a wide range of glyphs.

OpenType options

Perhaps you're working on a special project with lots of type, using an OpenType font that includes a ton of alternate characters, and you'd like to litter the text with the more unobtrusive characters (such as special ligatures like ᴔ, some swash glyphs like Q, or oldstyle numbers), but you don't have the hours available to select characters and replace them with glyphs from the Glyphs panel. The OpenType panel can automate this process (to a certain point).

TASK 10 Automatically replace glyphs with alternates

1 Select a range of type: With the black Selection tool, click on a text frame of either paragraph type or point type.

2 Open the OpenType panel: Choose Window > Type > OpenType.

The black-on-white icons at the bottom of the OpenType panel indicate *available* glyph options that are built into the currently selected font (see their tool tips). The gray-on-gray icons represent glyph options that are not available in the selected font (try another font!).

Glyph options.

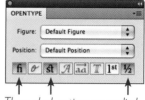

These glyph options are applied to the bottom example below.

The original OpenType type (Adobe Jenson Pro), without glyphs applied.

3 Apply the glyphs to your selected type: Click the glyph option icons you want to apply (the tool tips will tell you about each option).

The selected text updates to show the results (below).

first fluffy toy ½ off!

The glyphs that replaced ordinary characters are highlighted.

Tabs and indents

If you use the Spacebar to indent a paragraph or act as "tabs," or use the Return/Enter key to create extra space between paragraphs, STOP IT! These techniques create sloppy alignments and big gaps between paragraphs, and when you want to change the indents, fake tabs, and spacing, you have to change all those spaces and Returns manually. (Other than that, no problem.) Spend a few minutes learning to be more efficient (and more professional).

TASK 11 Create paragraph indents

A standard paragraph indent is *not* five spaces with the Spacebar. That is so half-a-century-ago typewriter mentality (even if you've never even seen a typewriter). A standard indent is about two spaces, the width of the point size of the type; 12-point type has a 12-point indent.

1 Type several paragraphs in a text frame: Let the text bump into the edge of the text frame and wrap to the next line. When you want a new paragraph, hit ONE Return/Enter.

Use the black Selection tool to select the type frame. The tab and indent settings **will affect all paragraphs in the frame.**

To affect only one paragraph, click in it with the Type tool.

To affect multiple paragraphs, click anywhere in one, then press-and-drag to select all or part of *adjacent* paragraphs.

2 Open the Tabs panel: Choose Window > Type > Tabs.

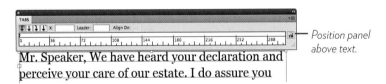

— Position panel above text.

The Tabs panel opens directly above and aligned to the selected type frame. (If it's not aligned, click the magnet icon on the right side of the panel to make it snap to the frame.)

TIP: To get a specific amount of space between paragraphs, use the **Paragraph Space After** field shown on page 131.

Highlighted below are two indent markers. The **top marker** indents the **first line in a paragraph**; the **bottom marker** sets the left indent of **all the rest of the lines in a paragraph.**

Indent markers.

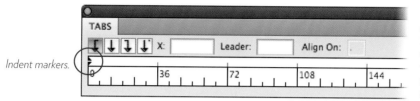

*There is also a **right indent marker** on the far right end of the Tabs ruler, which aligns with the right edge of the text frame.*

3 **Indent the *first line*** (below, left): Drag the top indent marker to the right. A vertical line appears as you drag as a visual guide. When you let go, the first line snaps to the indent position.

4 **Indent *all other lines* of the paragraph** (below, right): Drag the bottom indent marker to the right. Let go when the vertical black line is where you want the indent positioned.

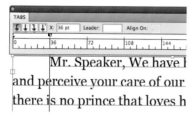

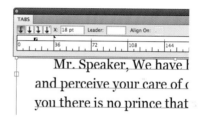

5 **Create a hanging indent** (below, left): Leave the top indent marker in the far-left position; drag the bottom indent marker to the right to indent all lines of type *except* the first line.

6 **Indent *all* lines of type** (below, right): First, align both indent markers together. Then, **to drag the markers together,** hold down the Command key (PC: Control key) as you drag.

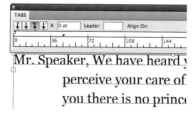

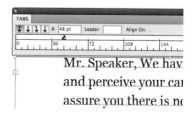

TASK 12   Create and use tab stops

When you have multiple columns of information to align, use tabs. After you've created the tab stops you need, you can always drag the tab stops to make changes when necessary.

The Tabs panel ruler has invisible default tabs set at every half-inch, so when you hit the Tab key, the insertion point moves to the next half-inch mark it can reach. Those settings are never what you want, so you just need to learn how to customize them.

The close-up below highlights the four types of tab stops; Illustrator calls them Left-Justified, Center-Justified, Right-Justified, and Decimal-Justified.

Tab stops.—
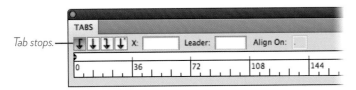

1   Create some text similar to the example below.

After typing each item, hit the Tab key instead of the Spacebar.

The text is jumping to Illustrator's hidden, default tab markers, which is not what you want, but don't worry—you'll override those markers with your own, in Step 3. Right now we just want to make sure that each piece of text has been told to go to a marker.

| Much ToDo | Too long | Long ago | Mary | $9,999.99 |
| Hamlit Even longer | 15-something | Fred | 00.99 | |

2   It's often helpful to *see* the hidden characters, such as tabs and spaces, as shown below. **To show hidden characters,** choose Type > Show Hidden Characters.

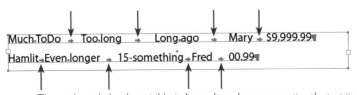

These tab symbols, when visible, indicate that tabs are separating the text items. The text is aligning with the tab marker you sent it to.

TIP: If you have rulers showing in your document, understand that the Tabs panel ruler **has nothing whatsoever to do with the document rulers!** The Tabs ruler measures each text frame *separately.*

3   Open the Tabs panel: Choose Window > Type > Tabs.

The Tabs panel positions itself above the text *in which the insertion point is flashing.*

4   With the Type tool, drag to highlight the two lines of text because the settings in the Tabs panel apply to *selected* paragraphs.

5   Select the "Left-Justified Tab" (shown to the left), then click the position in the ruler at the point where you want the *second* column of items to align (since the *first* column of items has no tab marker attached, and the column sits at the left *margin*).

6   Next, click farther to the right where the *third* column should align, and then set a tab marker for the *fourth* column.

As you set left-justified tab markers, you can see the items move over to snap into alignment with the markers.

7   For the last column ($9,999.99), choose the "Decimal-Justified Tab" icon (shown to the left), then click the ruler approximately where you think the decimals should line up (widen your text frame if necessary).

8   Don't forget, after you set the tab markers, you can drag them left or right to fine-tune the column alignments.

Once you've got tabs set up, click (with the Type tool) at the end of the last word, hit a Return/Enter, and continue to create more columns. The tab settings you created will carry on as long as you keep hitting Returns.

Left-justified tabs.   *Decimal-justified tab.*

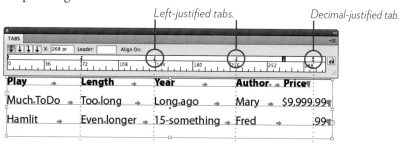

The dotted lines are just to show the vertical alignment created by tabs.

TIP: The Tabs ruler displays the measurement unit that is set in the Preferences, under "Units," which you can change at any time.

You can also **change the measurement units** on the fly: In a document, make sure the rulers are showing (Command R/PC: Control R). Right-click in a ruler and choose the measurement units you would like to use. This also changes the units in the Tabs ruler.

Paragraph and Character style sheets

When a project requires a lot of text formatting, you can save a great deal of time and ensure consistency by creating *paragraph* and *character style sheets*. A style sheet is a collection of formatting specifications that you can apply with a single click; when you want to change the formatting on the page, you change the style sheet definition, and everything that has that style applied changes automatically. This is truly wonderful, and this chapter is truly a very *brief* introduction to this powerful feature.

Paragraph style sheets

Paragraph style sheets apply to **entire paragraphs**—things like alignment, linespacing, tracking, paragraph spacing, tabs, indents, etc. Anything you can set in the Paragraph panel (except kerning) can be used in a paragraph style definition.

As usual, to apply paragraph-level formatting you only need to click in a paragraph to select it. You can select a number of text frames with the black Selection tool and also apply paragraph formatting (including paragraph style sheets) to all the text in the frames.

Every piece of text in this entire book has a style sheet applied.

TASK 13   Create and use a paragraph style

Create a new style using the Paragraph Styles panel

If you know at least approximately what you want the text to look like, you can go straight to the Paragraph Styles panel and set it up.

1   Open the Paragraph Styles panel: Choose Window > Type > Paragraph Styles.

2   Create a new paragraph style: Click the *Create New Style* button at the bottom of the panel.

Create New Style.

3   A new style appears in the panel named "Paragraph Style 1." Double-click that name to open the "Paragraph Style Options" shown at the top of the opposite page.

4 Name the style something that will make it clear to you what it is for when you later see it in a lengthy list of styles!

5 Select a formatting heading on the left to set the options for it on the right. You don't have to set something for every field—just choose options that you know you want.

6 Click OK, and that style sheet name appears in the panel.

Create a new style from existing text

But perhaps some text is already on the page and you've formatted it visually; now it's perfect and you want to turn that into a style sheet.

7 With the Type tool, click in the formatted text.

8 In the Paragraph Styles panel, click the *Create New Style* button.

9 Double-click the new style that appears in the panel, named "Paragraph Style 2" (or some other number).

10 In the options dialog box, shown above, name the style and click OK.

Apply a paragraph style to text

11 With the Type tool, click in a paragraph to select it, *or* press-and-drag to select more than one paragraph, *or* use the black Selection tool to select one or more text frames.

12 With the text selected, click the style name in the Paragraph Style panel. The formatting is applied to the selection, and that text is now considered tagged with a style sheet.

Edit a paragraph style

When you edit the style sheet, the changes will apply to every paragraph that is tagged with this style. This is a good thing. In fact, this is the point!

13 Double-click the style name in the Paragraph Styles panel. In the "Paragraph Style Options" dialog box that opens, make your changes. Click OK and everything updates!

Character style sheets

Character style sheets apply to **selected characters**; any settings in the Character panel can be used. The bold characters that you see in this paragraph and throughout the book were created using a character style sheet. If I want every bold setting like that in the entire book changed to red italic, I can do it with a click of the button in the style sheet definition. Amazing.

Paragraph style sheets, as you learned on the previous pages, apply to entire paragraphs. Character style sheets can override the paragraph style sheet for selected characters, so you can use both in the same paragraph, as shown above.

You can create a style sheet from scratch, as explained in Steps 1–6, or format the text first, then use that to define a new style sheet, as explained in Steps 7–10.

TASK 14   Create and use a character style

Create a new style using the Character Styles panel

If you know at least approximately what you want the text to look like, you can go straight to the Character Styles panel and set it up.

1   Open the Character Styles panel: Choose Window > Type > Character Styles.

2   Create a new character style: Click the *Create New Style* button at the bottom of the panel.

Create New Style.

3   A new style appears in the panel named "Character Style 1." Double-click that name to open the "Character Style Options" shown below.

You don't have to fill in every field. Any field left blank will retain the settings of the original text.

For instance, if I don't enter a leading value, the character style will use the leading value of the current text. That's good.

4 Name the style something that will make it clear to you what it is for when you later see it in a lengthy list of styles!

5 Select a formatting heading on the left to set the options for it on the right. You don't have to set something for every field— any field left blank will pick up the formatting of the current text.

6 Click OK, and that style sheet name appears in the panel.

Create a new style from existing text

But perhaps some text is already on the page and you've formatted it visually; now it's perfect and you want to turn that into a style sheet.

7 With the Type tool, click in the formatted text.

8 In the Character Styles panel, click the *Create New Style* button.

9 Double-click the new style that appears in the panel, named "Character Style 2" (or some other number).

10 In the Options dialog box, shown opposite, name the style and click OK.

Apply a character style to text

11 With the Type tool, press-and-drag to select the characters to which you want to apply the style sheet.

12 With the text selected, click the style name in the Character Style panel. The formatting is applied to the selection, and that text is now considered tagged with a style sheet.

The first known mermaid stories appeared in Assyria around 1000 BCE. The goddess Atargatis, mother of Assyrian queen Semiramis, loved a mortal shepherd and unintentionally killed him. Ashamed, she jumped into a lake to take the form of a fish, but the waters would not conceal her divine beauty. Thereafter, she took the form of a mermaid—human above the waist, fish below.

The Greeks recognized Atargatis under the name Derketo. Prior to 546 BCE, the Milesian philosopher Anaximander proposed that mankind had sprung from an aquatic species of animal. He thought that humans, with their extended infancy, could not have survived otherwise.

A popular Greek legend turns Alexander the Great's sister, Thessalonike, into a mermaid after she died. She lived, it was said, in the Aegean and when she encoun- tered a ship, she asked its sailors only one question: "Is

This is a simple example of character styles applied in text.

At any point, you can edit the style sheet (Step 13) and everything that has been tagged with that style will instantly update with the changes.

Edit a character style

When you edit the style sheet, the changes will apply to every character that is tagged with this style. This is a good thing. In fact, this is the point!

13 Double-click the style name in the Character Styles panel. In the "Character Style Options" dialog box that opens, make your changes. Click OK and everything updates!

141

Modify type objects

The ability to modify type is one of the main reasons to use Illustrator. It's great for logo projects because it's so easy to customize the look to make it unique. Type can be treated not only as text, but as an object. To get the basic idea of how to modify type, follow along in this task and build yourself a logo.

TASK 15   Format the basic text

1   Set some type for a logo, such as below. Include two words and an ampersand (&), no spaces. I used 72-point Georgia just to get started.

Falstaff&Pistol

2   **Change the font:** Use the *Font* pop-up menu in the Control panel. I chose Fette Fraktur, but use anything you like.

𝕱𝖆𝖑𝖘𝖙𝖆𝖋𝖋&𝕻𝖎𝖘𝖙𝖔𝖑

3   **Select the ampersand:** With the Type tool, drag to select it (shown, below).

4   **Change the font size:** In the *Font Size* field in the Control panel, type a value of 150 point.

This ampersand is selected and enlarged.

5   With the ampersand still selected (highlighted), **change its color:** Click the *Font Color* pop-up menu in the Control panel, then choose a purple color swatch. The ampersand changes to a purple fill.

Change the color of any other type you want: Drag across it to select it, then choose a fill color in the Control panel.

6   **Remove any extra space** that might be trapped between the giant ampersand and the letter to its right (this will depend on the font and the combination of letters you chose): With the Type tool, click between the "&" and the "P" (shown at the top of the opposite page).

*The Type tool sets a blinking **insertion point**.* →

7   Click the word "Character" in the Control panel to open the
Character panel, then enter a value of -150 in the Kerning field (you
might need a different value, depending on the letter combination).

*This kerning value affects
the spacing between two
characters (see page 130
for more on kerning).*

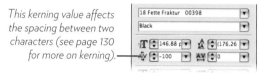

TASK 16   Modify the type object shape

The formatting you did in the first seven steps was nothing new. But a
great thing about Illustrator is that you can also affect the text as an object.

1   **To select the type as an object,** use the black Selection tool. A bounding
box with corner and side handles appears around the type.

2   **To distort the proportions** of the type object, hover the black Selection
tool over a *corner* handle. When the cursor changes into a double-
arrow, drag in any direction.

To resize the type object proportionately, hold down the Shift key
as you drag.

3   **To condense the type width** (but keep the height the same), hover the
black Selection tool over a *side* handle. When the cursor changes into
a double-arrow (circled below), drag inward, toward the center.

To widen the type (but keep the height the same), drag outward.

To reduce the height (but keep the width the same), drag the *top* or
bottom handle toward the center. **To enlarge the height** of the type,
drag outward.

*The pointer
changes into a
double-arrow
when you hover
over a corner
or side handle.*

TASK 17   Warp the type object

1   If you created a type object in Task 15, select it with the black Selection tool (if you didn't create one, do so now).

2   In the Control panel, find the "Make Envelope" icon (shown above) in the Control panel. Click the triangle on the right side of the icon to open its little menu, and choose "Make With Warp…."

3   Click the "Preview" checkbox so you can see the results of your settings as you experiment.

4   In the "Warp Options" dialog box that opens, choose "Arc" from the "Style" pop-up menu.

   (Also experiment with the other style options, and try it sometime with a few paragraphs of text.)

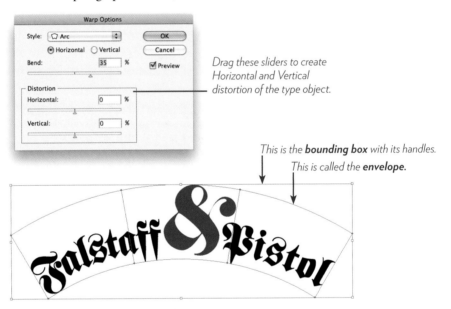

Drag these sliders to create Horizontal and Vertical distortion of the type object.

*This is the **bounding box** with its handles.*
*This is called the **envelope**.*

ABOVE: The type object with the settings shown above in the Warp Options dialog box.

BELOW: The same type object with "Bend" set to -24%, horizontal distortion set to -35%, and vertical distortion set to 22%.

5   Move the "Bend" slider to 35%. Click OK.

6   Now let's get really weird, typographically speaking—let's edit the envelope (see the callout on the opposite page for *envelope*).

    With the white Direct Selection tool, click an anchor point on the envelope (shown circled below).

    Drag the anchor point to another position to reshape it.
    Drag a direction handle to reshape it.

> **TIP:** To create more uniform distortion (is that an oxymoron?), marquee around two connected points (or Shift-click them), top and bottom, so they reshape in unison with each other.

7   **Edit the type in its distorted envelope:** With the black Selection tool, select the object. Click the "Edit Contents" icon in the Control panel.

Edit Envelope. ———— *Edit Contents.*

8   Choose the Type tool; move the Type tool over the object. The original, unwarped text appears in whatever color is assigned to the object's layer (see Chapter 9 on layers).

    Click within the type *or* drag to select characters, then make editing changes. Choose the black Selection tool to see the changes.

9   **To make the graphic independent of the font** so you don't need to include the font every time you want to use the logo, **convert it to outlines.** Keep in mind that once you do this, the type is no longer editable as text! You will, however, now have anchor points that you can manipulate with the white Direct Selection tool.

    To convert to outlines, select the object, then choose Object > Expand….

Try this!

Create a postcard, a flyer, or CD cover using only type—no graphics or art. Use the tools in Illustrator to create an artful, typographic piece with visual interest. Don't forget about the brush effect techniques on pages 80–81. It always helps, of course, to have some interesting fonts on hand; check MyFonts.com for inexpensive ones.

11 Color and Gradients

How amazing it is to have unlimited colors just a click away. *And* control such as has never before been seen on Earth. Illustrator provides you with an amazing amount of control over accessing, creating, organizing, and managing color groups, color libraries, global colors, CMYK and RGB, custom gradients, color harmonies, and more.

Hue Harmony: Notorious Swatchbuckler.

From the *16TH CENTURY PIONEERS OF VECTOR ARTWORK* series.

Ways to apply color

When you select a color, it is applied to the *active* **attribute of the selected object**—either the *fill* or *stroke* attribute, whichever is the foremost icon in the Tools panel, below (or Color panel, shown opposite). This is really important to understand and hard to remember. We've been selecting colors for many years and still forget to choose the attribute first—we constantly end up surprised at what changed color. Sheesh.

To switch fill and stroke colors, click here.
Or press **Shift X.**

Fill color box. ——
Stroke color box. ——

When the fill color box is in front, it is the active attribute.
To switch the active attributes, press **X.**

TASK 1 Use the Color Picker to apply a color

1 Open the Color Picker: Double-click the fill or stroke color box in the Tools panel or in the Color panel.

2 To change the hue (the color) in the color field on the left, drag the sliders *or* click inside the vertical color spectrum bar.

Drag the circular marker in the color field to change the hue's saturation (more or less color, drag left and right) and brightness (more or less white, drag up or down).

3 Click OK to place the new color in both the Tools panel and the Color panel.

New color.
Original color.
Color marker in the color field.

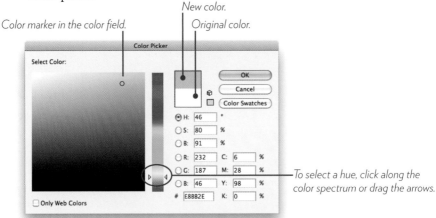

To select a hue, click along the color spectrum or drag the arrows.

If you know the numerical values of the color you want to use, type them into the appropriate color model fields. The color models are HSB (Hue, Saturation, Brightness, useful for adjusting colors, as above), RGB (Red, Green, Blue, for screen graphics), and CMYK (Cyan, Magenta, Yellow, Black, for print graphics).

TASK 2 Use the Swatches panel to apply color

The Swatches panel is where you choose most colors, because it's where you also collect colors to use in a project. See pages 152–156 for lots more about the Swatches panel.

- Select an object, then click a color swatch in the Swatches panel. The swatch color is applied to the object's *active* attribute (either the fill or the stroke, as explained on the opposite page).

- *Or* drag a color from the Swatches panel and drop it on top of an object, even if it's unselected. The color is applied to the object's *active* attribute.

TASK 3 Use the Color panel to apply color

The Color panel provides sliders to edit a color. This panel allows you to choose an attribute (the fill or stroke) to make it *active*.

1 Open the Color panel: Choose Window > Color.

2 Drag the color sliders to edit the current color.

   Or click in the spectrum bar to select a general hue, then modify the color with the sliders.

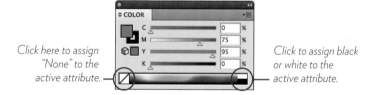

Click here to assign "None" to the active attribute.

Click to assign black or white to the active attribute.

3 **To add a color to the current Swatch collection,** drag the fill or stroke color box from the Color panel and drop it in the Swatches panel.

   Or click the Color panel menu in the top-right corner of the panel; choose "Create New Swatch." In the "New Swatch" dialog box (below), you can edit the color, name it, and choose a color model.

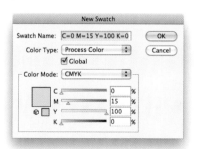

NOTE: "White" is opaque. "None" is not white—it's transparent.

Select and apply color with the Eyedropper tool

You can "load" the eyedropper with color (and formatting) from one object (or text) and apply that to another object (or text). What exactly gets loaded is determined by the "Eyedropper Options"—double-click the Eyedropper tool to view and change those options.

There are two ways to use the Eyedropper, and if you don't understand this about the tool, it will make you crazy. Repeat these tasks until you feel comfortable and can predict what will happen when you click.

TASK 4   Apply color or formatting to a selected object

If an object is selected and you click on another object with the Eyedropper tool, the attributes that you click on are applied to the selected object.

1   Create two shapes; give them different stroke colors and weights and different fill colors.

2   With the black Selection tool, select one shape.

 3   With the Eyedropper tool, click on the second shape. The attributes from the second shape are applied to the first shape.

Repeat that a few times until you feel you've got it down.

TASK 5   Pick up formatting and drop it somewhere else

If nothing is selected, you can click on an object with the Eyedropper tool to *pick up* the attributes from that object, then apply those attributes to another object.

1   Create two shapes; give them different stroke colors and weights and different fill colors.

2   Choose the Eyedropper tool.

3   With the Eyedropper tool, click an object.

The object's fill and stroke colors appear in the fill and stroke color boxes in the Tools panel (and in the Color panel). Also, these attributes are **loaded** into the Eyedropper tool itself; it now looks like it's filled with something.

 This is a loaded Eyedropper. It is loaded with the attributes that are checked in the "Eyedropper Options" dialog box, opposite.

4   Apply those attributes to another object: Hold down the Option key (PC: Alt key) and single-click on another object. The Eyedropper *unloads* the attributes *into* the object you click.

Repeat the two methods until you understand what the Eyedropper tool is doing and how to control it.

TASK 6   Use the Eyedropper tool on type

1   Create two separate lines of point type (see page 123). Format them differently—different colors, fonts, styles, alignments, etc.

2   Use the methods in both Tasks 4 and 5 to match the attributes.

TIP: You're not limited to picking up attributes from similar objects; that is, you can pick up the color of text and apply it to an object, and vice versa. Experiment with this!

The Swatches panel

The Swatches panel is where you can keep colors you might want to use again. You can add new colors, delete colors, create color groups, save swatch collections, access many color libraries, and more.

Swatches panel overview

When you open a new document, the Swatches panel contains the default color swatches shown below: a rainbow assortment of solid color swatches, four gradient swatches, a pattern swatch, and two color groups (folders). These are meant to act as a starting point. You can customize the Swatches panel as much as you want, including how large the swatches appear in the panel (click the Swatches panel menu, then choose a small, medium, or large "Thumbnail View").

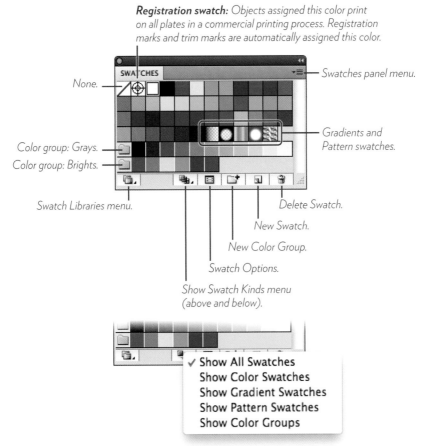

Registration swatch: *Objects assigned this color print on all plates in a commercial printing process. Registration marks and trim marks are automatically assigned this color.*

None.

Swatches panel menu.

Color group: Grays.
Color group: Brights.

Gradients and Pattern swatches.

Swatch Libraries menu.

Delete Swatch.

New Swatch.

New Color Group.

Swatch Options.

Show Swatch Kinds menu (above and below).

✓ Show All Swatches
Show Color Swatches
Show Gradient Swatches
Show Pattern Swatches
Show Color Groups

To simplify the appearance of the Swatches panel, *choose to show just the kind of swatches you need for the project at hand.*

TASK 7 Create new swatches

1   Open the Swatches panel: Choose Window > Swatches.

2   Click the *New Swatch* icon at the bottom of the panel; this opens the "New Swatch" dialog box.

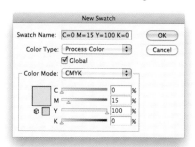

3   The "Swatch Name" is shown as ink color values. **Rename** the swatch color something like "Star Gold" or whatever makes sense to you (the ink values are still visible in the "Color Mode" section).

4   Choose a "Color Type" of "Process Color" (because this book is print-oriented; if you are creating work for a screen, use RGB).

5   Click the "Global" checkbox if you want the color to be **global.**

    If a color is global, that means if you make changes to it (such as make it darker or lighter), *all* instances of that color are changed automatically. For instance, let's say you made a sage green color and used it in seventeen objects throughout a poster. If you edit that sage green *global* color and make it lime green, each of those seventeen objects changes to lime green automatically. Try it—global colors act like style sheets. This is hugely useful, but you must be aware of the potential for changing the colors of objects that you didn't mean to.

    *A **white corner** identifies **global colors** in the Swatches panel.*

    If a color is **nonglobal, or local,** only *selected* objects will be affected when you edit the color. This is great because you can change an individual object without having to worry about other objects.

6   Click OK.

> **TIP:** You can use the Color panel to edit a color in a selected object, even if that color is a global one. Once you edit the color inside the object, however, it is no longer attached to the global swatch. This is not necessarily a bad thing—you can take advantage of it.

TASK 8 Edit a swatch color

1 Double-click a swatch in the Swatches panel.
Or select a swatch, then click the "Swatch Options' icon at the bottom of the panel (see page 152).

2 In the "Swatch Options" dialog box that opens (it's identical to the "New Swatch" dialog box on the previous page), adjust the color or make changes to any of the other options provided.

3 Click OK.

TIP: When editing an existing color swatch, you might want to duplicate the swatch first, then edit the duplicate: Choose "Duplicate Swatch" from the Swatches panel. This way you don't lose the original color, in case it has been applied to an object.

TASK 9 Create color groups

Organizing colors into groups helps manage large swatch collections and makes it easier to find the color you want.

1 Open the Swatches panel.

2 To open the "New Color Group" dialog box, click the *New Color Group* icon at the bottom of the panel.

3 Name the new group, then click OK.

4 A new color group folder appears in the Swatches panel. Drag swatches into the folder.

5 **To remove a swatch** from the color group, drag it out of the color group folder and drop it in the main swatches area or into another group folder.

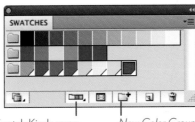

This Show Swatch Kinds *menu is set to "Show Color Groups." A folder of swatches is a color group.*

New Color Group.

TIP: To automatically create a new color group with swatches of your choice, select the swatches first, then click the *New Color Group* button.

TASK 10 Add colors from artwork to the Swatches panel

To add colors from existing artwork to the Swatches panel, do one of the following:

- Copy one or more objects from another document and paste them into the current document. The colors of the pasted objects automatically appear in the Swatches panel.

- To add *all document colors* that are not already in the Swatches panel (nonglobal, or local colors; see page 153), first deselect everything. From the Swatches panel menu, choose "Add Used Colors."

- To add color from a *selected* object, go to the Swatches panel menu and choose "Add Selected Colors."

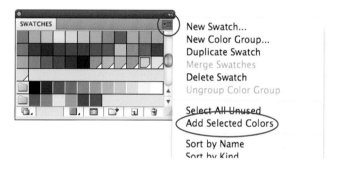

TASK 11 Open swatch libraries

Instead of spending time to create a lot of custom colors, explore the many swatch libraries provided.

1 Click the "Swatch Libraries" icon in the bottom left-corner of the Swatches panel.

2 Select one of the libraries, such as Art History > Russian Poster Art *or* Patterns > Nature > Animal Skins.

3 Click a color swatch in the new library panel that opens to add it to the Swatches panel.

TASK 12   Delete swatches you don't need

As you experiment with colors and gradients, your Swatches panel may fill up with unused swatches. **To remove swatches** from the panel, do one of the following:

- Select one or more swatches, then click the Trash icon in the lower-right corner of the panel.

- Select one or more swatches, then choose "Delete Swatch" from the Swatches panel menu.

- From the Swatches panel menu, choose "Select All Unused," then click the Trash icon.

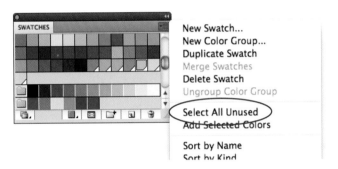

TASK 13   Share swatches with other applications

Once you've customized the Swatches panel to include just the swatches you need for a project, you can share that swatch collection with other Illustrator documents or with InDesign and Photoshop.

1   Make sure the Swatches panel includes the swatches you want, and delete the swatches you don't want to include.

2   From the Swatches panel menu, choose "Save Swatch Library as ASE…" (Adobe Swatch Exchange format), then name the swatch library. Save the file in Adobe Illustrator's Swatches folder.

3   To open the saved library, choose "Open Swatch Library > User Defined > *name-of-library.* The saved swatch library opens as a swatch library panel (it does not replace the current Swatches panel).

Recolor your artwork with a click

What a fabulous feature the "Recolor Artwork" dialog box is—you can create color variations of your artwork without spending more than five or ten seconds of your valuable time doing it.

TASK 14   Recolor artwork in the Edit pane

1   Use the black Selection tool to select some artwork.

 2   Click the *Recolor Artwork* button in the Control panel.

3   In the "Recolor Artwork" dialog box that opens, click the "Edit" tab.

4   Make sure the "Recolor Art" box is checked (bottom-left corner of the dialog box).

5   **To make all colors** in the document (represented by circular markers) move in harmonic unison with each other, click the *Link harmony colors* button in the lower-right corner of the color wheel.

To edit colors individually, click again to *Unlink harmony colors.*

6   Drag the large, black, circular marker to move all markers, and be amazed as the artwork is recolored.

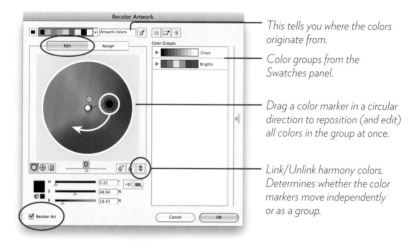

This tells you where the colors originate from.

Color groups from the Swatches panel.

Drag a color marker in a circular direction to reposition (and edit) all colors in the group at once.

Link/Unlink harmony colors. Determines whether the color markers move independently or as a group.

The artwork's original colors.   *The artwork's edited colors.*

TASK 15 Recolor artwork in the Assign pane

Before you start this task, select the Star tool and draw three stars. Assign a thick stroke weight, then assign various fill and stroke colors, as shown. *Or* create any simple, multicolored art.

1 Select the artwork.

 2 Click the *Recolor Artwork* button in the Control panel.

3 In the "Recolor Artwork" dialog box, click the "Assign" tab.

4 Click the *Get colors from selected art* button. The colors in the selected art appear in the active colors field.

5 Click the *Random color order* button: The same colors are used, but swapped with other colors in the artwork. When you stumble upon a combination you like, click OK.

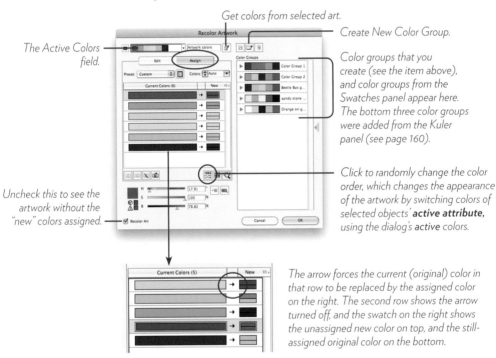

6 To put another group of colors in the *Active Colors* field, choose a color group from the "Color Groups" list.

TIP: If you don't see the "Assign" tab, it's because no artwork was selected when you opened this dialog box.

*Random color orders assigned,
with the fill attribute made active.*

*Random color orders assigned,
with the stroke attribute made active.*

7 Create a new color group from the active colors: Click the *New Color Group* button. The colors are added to the Colors Group list.

Try the Color Guide panel

Create harmonious color variations and save them to the Swatches panel.

TASK 16 Create color variations with the Color Guide panel

1 Open the Color Guide panel: Choose Window > Color Guide.

The group of colors in the top field represents a color *harmony rule* based on the color currently selected in the document.

2 Choose another harmony rule: Click the triangle on the right side of the *Harmony Rules* field to open a list of other harmony rules based on the existing colors. Choose a rule from the list.

3 Create variations of the colors in the harmony rule: Open the Color Guide panel menu, then choose the type of color variations to show (Tints/Shades, Warm/Cool, or Vivid/Muted).

The base colors are in the middle column, under the triangle, with variations on the left and right sides. To see a new harmony rule based on a color in the pane, click a color swatch in that pane, then click the tiny swatch to the left of the *Harmony Rules* field.

4 To add the harmonized color group to your Swatches panel, click the *Save color group* button in the bottom-right corner of the panel.

5 To apply any color in the panel to a *selected* object, click the color.

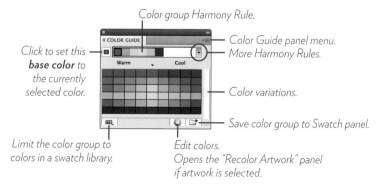

Color group Harmony Rule.

*Click to set this **base color** to the currently selected color.*

*Color Guide panel menu.
More Harmony Rules.*

Color variations.

Save color group to Swatch panel.

Limit the color group to colors in a swatch library.

*Edit colors.
Opens the "Recolor Artwork" panel if artwork is selected.*

The Kuler panel

The Kuler panel is another powerful solution to quickly create color groups for your Swatches panel. When you open the Kuler panel (below), it connects automatically (if you have an Internet connection) to an online resource of ready-to-use color harmony groups created by an online community of designers.

TASK 17   Add Kuler colors to the Swatches panel

1   Open the Kuler panel: Choose Window > Extensions > Kuler (the "Extensions" option is toward the top of the menu).

2   Click the left pop-up menu to choose which themes to display, based on criteria such as "highest rated" and "most popular."

3   Click the right pop-up menu to limit themes by their creation date.

4   Select a theme.

5   Save the theme to the Swatches panel: Click the *Add selected theme to swatches* button at the bottom of the Kuler panel.

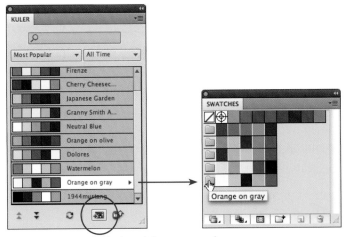

Add selected theme to swatches.

Color gradients

Color gradients can make plain graphics (shapes, illustrations, or type) appear more sophisticated and visually more interesting. Add to that the ease with which you can create great-looking gradients and you're in a transcendent state of gradient nirvana. Ommmmm (cue the background sitar music).

TASK 18   Create a color gradient

1   Select the Star tool and draw a star shape, such as the one below, left. I assigned this shape an orange fill and a 12-point stroke.

2   Open the **Gradient panel:** Choose Window > Gradient.

Click the gradient thumbnail to fill the star shape with that gradient.

If you don't see a **color stop** (as shown below) on the left side, just below the gradient bar, click in that position to create one.

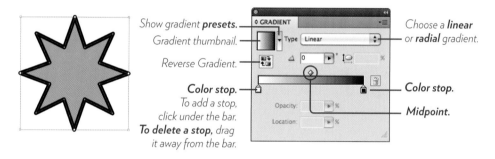

Show gradient **presets.**
Gradient thumbnail.
Reverse Gradient.

Color stop.
To add a stop, click under the bar.
To delete a stop, drag it away from the bar.

Choose a **linear** or **radial** gradient.

Color stop.

Midpoint.

3   **Create a new gradient *starting color:*** Double-click the starting *color stop* (under the left side of the gradient bar). In the color pop-up panel that opens (below, left), click the Swatches panel icon, then select a color for the color stop. To modify the color, click the Color panel icon (below, right).

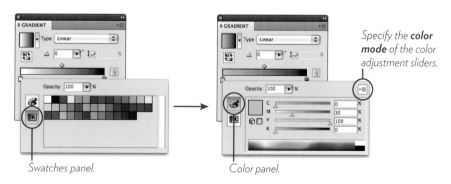

Swatches panel.

Color panel.

Specify the **color mode** of the color adjustment sliders.

To dismiss the panels shown above, click anywhere except the Gradient panel, *or* press the Escape key.

—continued

4   **Create a new gradient *ending color*:** Double-click the color stop located under the right side of the gradient bar.

In the panel that pops up, click the *Swatches* icon, then select an ending color for the gradient. When chosen, press Esc to close the pop-up panel, *or* click on any blank spot on the page.

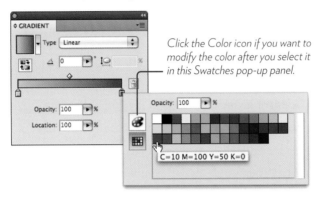

Click the Color icon if you want to modify the color after you select it in this Swatches pop-up panel.

5   **Change the proportions of the gradient colors:** With the star shape still selected, drag the *right* color stop to the left to increase the amount of that color in the gradient before it starts blending into the color on the right.

As you drag the slider, the midpoint automatically moves to maintain its position halfway between the two color stops, creating a smooth, even blend between the two stops—to change that behavior, drag the midpoint.

Drag the starting color stop.   *The gradient changes appear in the shape's fill.*

6   **Make sure the gradient type is Linear:** If your gradient is already Linear, skip to Step 7. If it's Radial, go to the Gradient panel "Type" menu and choose "Linear." This is just to ensure that the next step shows off its potential (it looks better in a linear gradient).

7 **Change the gradient angle:** Click the Gradient tool in the Tools panel.

The Gradient Annotator (or gradient slider) appears on top of the selected shape. When you hover the pointer over the Annotator, the same color stops and midway markers appear that you saw in the Gradient panel. You can drag to adjust them, right on top of the selected object, instead of using the Gradient panel. That's cool.

Hover the pointer just barely past the *right* end (the end with a diamond on it) of the Gradient Annotator line. When the pointer changes to a rotate icon (below, right—*not* the square icon), drag in a circular motion to rotate the Annotator. The gradient blend updates when you release the Annotator.

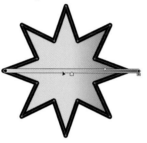 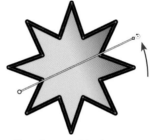

The Gradient Annotator. *Drag the end of the Annotator to rotate the gradient.*

8 **Create a more dramatic radial gradient:** Change the gradient to "Radial" in the "Type" pop-up menu (Step 6).

Choose the Gradient tool (if it's not already chosen) to show the Gradient Annotator on top of the shape.

To add a new color stop: Hover the pointer along the bottom edge of the Annotator until the cursor adds a plus sign (below, left); click to add a new color stop (add it toward the left edge).

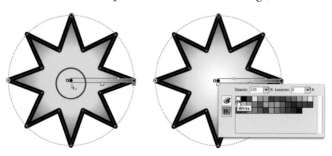

Double-click the new color stop. In the panel that pops up, select the white swatch (above, right).

—continued

Drag the *ending* color stop toward the left, to move the ending color closer to the middle of the shape (below, left).

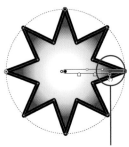 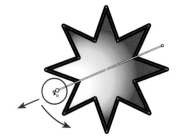

Drag this color stop toward the left.　　　*Drag left and counterclockwise.*

9　**To stretch the Annotator** and move the gradient center away from the shape's center (above, right), drag the *left* end of the gradient bar (the center of the radial gradient). *At the same time,* drag in a clockwise or counterclockwise direction to rotate the gradient to the lower-left section of the star shape.

10　**To change the radial gradient's circular shape to an ellipse,** hover the pointer over the boundary area of the radial shape to display its path (below). Drag the *solid black dot* inward or outward; drag the *outlined dot* to enlarge or reduce the size of the path. Notice how this affects the gradient.

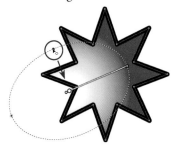 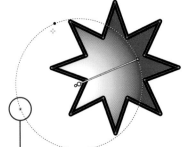

Drag the black dot to change the gradient's shape.　　　*Drag the outlined dot to enlarge or reduce the size of the gradient path.*

11　**Add the gradient to the Swatches panel** so you can use it again: Open the Swatches panel. Drag the gradient thumbnail from the Gradient panel into the Swatches panel.

　　Or click the triangle button next to the gradient thumbnail in the Gradient panel. At the bottom of the panel that pops up, click the *Add to Swatches* button (the icon looks like a floppy disk from the previous century—kinda weird).

12 **Reverse the gradient:** Select the object, then click the *Reverse Gradient* button in the Gradient panel.

Reverse Gradient.

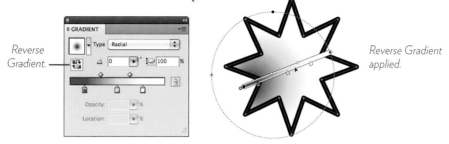

Reverse Gradient applied.

13 **Change the opacity in the gradient:** First, get the Rectangle tool and draw a rectangle filled with blue. Place the rectangle behind the star, as shown below (select the rectangle, then choose Object > Arrange > Send to Back).

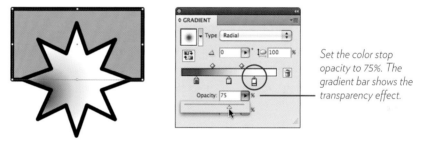

Set the color stop opacity to 75%. The gradient bar shows the transparency effect.

With the black Selection tool, select the star shape. In the Gradient panel, click the white color stop (circled, above-right). Set the "Opacity" slider to 75%. The result is shown below, left.

You can **load a library of preset gradients:** Click the *Swatch Libraries* button in the bottom-left corner of the Swatches panel. Choose "Gradients," then choose from a sizeable list of preset gradients, a couple of which are shown to the right.

Try this!

Use shape tools, line tools, the Pen tool, and the Blob brush to draw a Picasso-inspired face. Goofy and ugly scores higher than photorealistic.

Assign different fill and stroke colors, including gradients (I used gradients from the Swatches Library menu; see Step 11 on page 164).

After you create a big mess (of strokes, shapes, fills, and gradients), adjust the colors using the "Recolor Artwork" dialog box (pages 157–159).

Section 4
Manipulate Objects

Ryan Williams, cofounder of and designer at
ForgedClothing.com, took a photo of a flag
on the wall of his Crossfit gym and imported it
into Illustrator where he traced it, cleaned it up
(straight lines for the stripes), and distressed it.

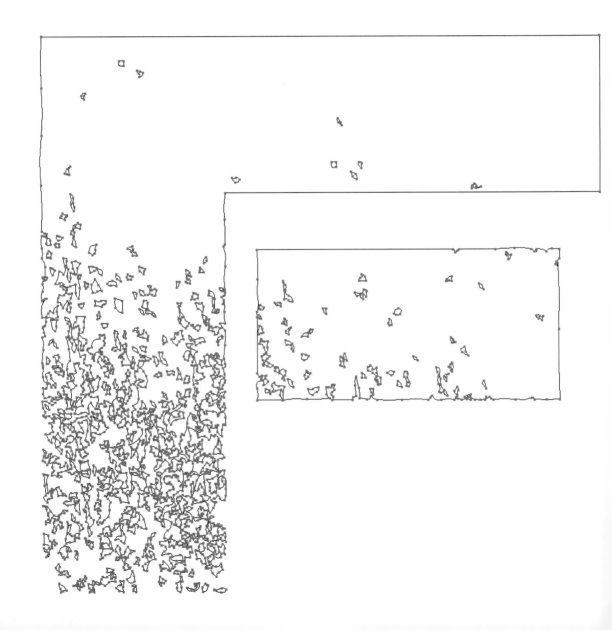

12 Transform and Modify

Once you've created an object of some sort, there are many ways to transform and modify it, and, as usual, there are multiple ways to do most things. As you carry out the tasks in this chapter, experiment with options and settings that are not specifically called for in the task. Working with Illustrator is an ongoing journey of exploration and discovery!

Transform objects

When you **transform** an object, it means you rotate, reflect, scale, shear, or distort it in some way.

The following tasks show you how to use the transform tools from the Tools panel and take advantage of the possibilities. You'll find yourself transforming objects constantly while you create art in Illustrator.

Rotate objects

Rotating an object is a task that is useful in almost every project.

TASK 1   Rotate an object using the Rotate tool

1   With the black Selection tool, select an object (or draw a new one). I used the Pen tool to draw the swash shape shown below.

Select the shape.   The rotation reference point.

2   With the shape selected (above, left), choose the Rotate tool in the Tools panel; single-click where you want to place the *center point* of the rotation, the reference point (above, right).

3   Move the pointer away from the reference point, then press-and-drag in a circular direction (as shown by the arrow, above-right).

TASK 2   Rotate an object using the "Rotate" dialog box

1   Double-click the Rotate tool in the Tools panel.

2   Click the "Preview" box, enter a value in the "Angle" field, then click OK.

To create a rotated copy and leave the original object unchanged, click "Copy."

TASK 3   Rotate an object using the bounding box

1   With the black Selection tool, click the shape you created in Task 1.

2   Hover the pointer near a corner point of the bounding box until you see the pointer change to a rotate icon (double curved arrow, below, left).

3   Drag to rotate the object (below, right).

   To make a duplicate, hold down the Option key (PC: Alt key) as you drag.

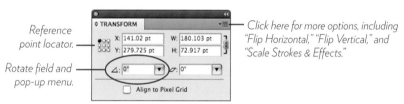

When the Selection tool pointer is near a corner, it changes to a rotate icon.

TASK 4   Rotate an object using the Transform panel

1   Select the shape you created in Task 1.

2   Open the Transform panel: Choose Window > Transform.

Reference point locator.

Click here for more options, including "Flip Horizontal," "Flip Vertical," and "Scale Strokes & Effects."

Rotate field and pop-up menu.

3   Set the rotation reference point: Click one of the squares in the *reference point locator* to determine the *center point* of rotation.

4   Click the "Rotate" pop-up menu and choose a preset rotation angle.

   Or enter a value in the Rotate field.

   Or with the value in the Rotate field selected (click the angle icon to select the field), tap the up and down arrow keys to rotate the object one degree with each tap. Hold down the Shift key as you tap an arrow key to rotate the object ten degrees with each tap.

TIP: To keep things tidy, you can reset the bounding box after you rotate an object: Choose Object > Transform > Reset Bounding Box.

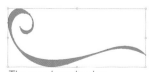

The rotated shape and bounding box.   *The reset bounding box.*

Reflect objects

When you **reflect** an object, you flip it across an axis. There are, as usual, several ways to do this.

TASK 5   Flip an object using the Reflect tool

Reflected objects are flipped across an invisible axis, usually horizontal or vertical. You can determine the axis, the origin point and angle of the reflection, and whether to reflect the original or a copy.

1   With the black Selection tool, select an object to reflect.

2   Choose the Reflect tool.

3   With the Reflect tool, click to set one point of the axis; for instance, click at the intersection of an invisible horizontal and vertical axis, as shown below. The location of the **first click** determines the point across which the object will flip. This first click also changes the pointer to an arrowhead icon.

4   The **second click** determines whether the object will be flipped across a horizontal or vertical axis. Click (your second click) directly *below* the first click to define a vertical axis—the object flips across the invisible vertical axis.

Flipped across the vertical axis.

Or click to the left or right of your first click to define a horizontal axis. The object flips across the invisible horizontal axis.

5   **Create a copy as you reflect** the object: Repeat Steps 1–3, then hold down the Option key (PC: Alt key) when you repeat Step 4.

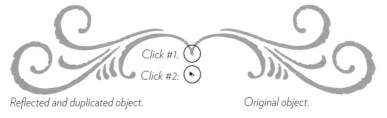

Reflected and duplicated object.   Original object.

6 **Reflect the object at an angle,** using the dialog box: Double-click the Reflect tool to open the "Reflect" dialog box.

Enter "20" (or any value you want) in the "Angle" text field. Click the "Preview" checkbox to see the result of your setting.

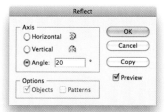

You can use this dialog box to reflect objects horizontally or vertically, but you won't be able to select the position of the reflection axis, as demonstrated on the previous page. The axis will automatically be the center of the object.

7 **Reflect the object visually:** Repeat Steps 1–3 on the previous page.

In Step 4, *drag* (don't click) the axis left or right to change its angle and the angle of the reflected object. The reflected version appears in outline mode as you drag (shown below).

To make a copy of the reflected object and leave the original unchanged, Option-drag (PC: Alt-drag) the axis.

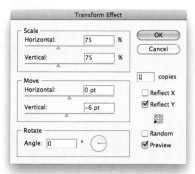

Click #1.

DISCOVERY: Experiment with the "Transform Effect" dialog box (Effect > Distort & Transform > Transform...) to reflect, move, and scale an object all at once. *Effects* do not alter the original object, and they can be changed or removed at any time—any effects you apply to an object appear in the Appearance panel (see page 186), where they can be modified.

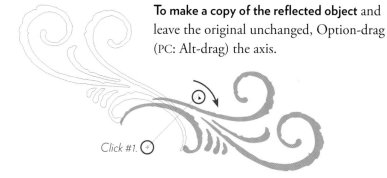

The reflected object above is also scaled to 75%, and moved –6 points.

Shear objects

The Shear tool slants an object along a horizontal or vertical axis, or along an angle you specify.

TASK 6 Slant an object using the Shear tool

1 Select an object or a grouped object.

2 Choose the Shear tool in the Tools panel.

3 Drag anywhere in the document to slant the object (below, left). Although you *can* drag anywhere in the document, it's easier to control the amount of slant if, before you drag, you position the pointer so it is *not* horizontally or vertically aligned with the Shear center point (the middle of the object, marked by crosshairs).

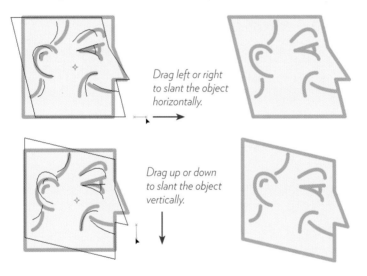

Drag left or right to slant the object horizontally.

Drag up or down to slant the object vertically.

TASK 7 Shear a line of type

1 Type a word or two of large, bold text, then select it with the black Selection tool.

2 With the Reflect tool, drag in the document.

3 Drag left or right to skew the type horizontally (below, left).

Or drag up or down to skew the type vertically (below, right).

As you drag, the transformed object appears in the color for that layer.

Scale (resize) and distort objects

You can scale objects manually by dragging; when you need more precise positioning, you can enter measurements into the "Scale" dialog box.

By default, strokes and effects applied to an object are *not* scaled along with the object. To change that default setting, on a Mac choose Illustrator > Preferences > General (PC choose Edit > Preferences > General), then select "Scale Strokes & Effects."

TASK 8   Scale an object using its bounding box

1   Select an object (the leaf object below was drawn with the Blob brush).

2   Hide the individual paths and points, as shown here, to make it easier to see the selection: Choose View > Hide Edges.

3   With the black Selection tool, hover the pointer over one of the handles on the bounding box. When the pointer changes to a double arrow, drag away from the center; to maintain the proportions, hold down the Shift key as you drag.

To enlarge or reduce the object from the center, add the Option key (PC: Alt key) as you drag.

TASK 9   Scale an object using the Scale dialog box

1   Select an object, then double-click the Scale tool in the Tools panel.

2   Enter values in either the "Uniform" or "Non-Uniform" sections.

3   Click OK.

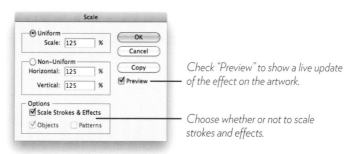

Check "Preview" to show a live update of the effect on the artwork.

Choose whether or not to scale strokes and effects.

TASK 10   Transform an object using the Transform panel

1   Select an object with the black Selection tool.

2   Open the Transform panel: Choose Window > Transform.

3   Click one of the squares in the reference point locator to determine the origin point of the transformation (shear, rotate, resize, move).

4   Enter values in the value fields.

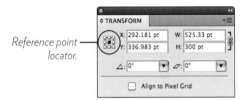

Reference point locator.

TASK 11   Use the Effect menu to distort artwork

The Effect menu contains some interesting distortions that you should explore. Meanwhile, as a sample, apply the "Roughen" effect to an object.

1   With the black Selection tool, select an object.

2   Choose Effect > Distort & Transform > Roughen….

3   Click "Preview" to see how your settings affect the artwork.

4   Experiment with the various settings in the "Roughen" dialog box.

5   When you're happy with the effect, click OK.

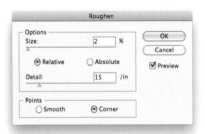

Roughen settings applied to artwork.

With the effect applied, the outline view shows that the original artwork is unchanged.

To access and edit the paths and points of the "roughened" version, you must **expand** the artwork (Object > Expand Appearance). However, expanded artwork can no longer be adjusted using the Effect menu.

TIP: Effects don't change the original artwork, so you can modify or remove an effect at any time.

TASK 12 Transform an object using the Free Transform tool

1 With the black Selection tool, select an object.

2 Choose the Free Transform tool in the Tools panel.

3 **To create a freeform distortion**, start dragging a corner handle of the bounding box, then hold down the Command key (PC: Control key) as you drag in any direction (below, left).

4 **To create a perspective distortion** (below, right), first undo the freeform distortion: Choose Edit > Undo Perspective (Illustrator calls the freeform distortion "perspective" in the menu).

   With the object selected, start dragging a corner handle, then hold down the Shift Option Command keys (PC: Shift Alt Control keys). Drag in various directions until you achieve the perspective you want.

TASK 13 Move an object using the Move dialog box

Most of the time when you want to move an object, you just select it and drag it. But in some situations, you may need to move one or more objects using very precise measurements. The Move dialog box enables you to do that.

1 Select an object, then double-click the black Selection tool (also known as the Move tool).

2 Click "Preview" so you can watch the results, then enter values into the "Horizontal" and "Vertical" value fields. Click OK.

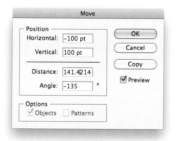

Slice and cut objects

The Eraser, Scissors, and Knife tool are bundled together in the Tools panel. They're extremely useful for modifying existing shapes and paths.

TASK 14   Use the Eraser tool to erase part of an object

The Eraser tool erases anything you drag it over.

1 Choose the Eraser tool.

2 Adjust the size of the Eraser tool to determine the size of an area to erase: Tap the right bracket to enlarge, tap the left bracket to reduce the size.

3 Drag across the object. **Whatever you drag across is erased** (below, left).

   To erase certain paths or shapes and nothing else, select those objects, then drag across them (below, right).

I erased a swath from the flowers.

I selected *one* of the flower fills, then went to the Select > Same > Fill & Stroke menu to select all the other flowers. As I erased, only the selected items disappeared.

Erase a complex object or a simple one. Illustrator automatically closes paths, as shown here.

TASK 15   Use the Scissors tool to modify a path

The Scissors tool splits a path or a shape.

1 Draw an open path and assign a thick stroke to it.

2 Choose the Scissors tool, then click anywhere on the path.

Click with the Scissors tool.

3 Get the black Selection tool, then select the highlighted path segment and drag it to another position.

4 As another example, this time draw a *closed path,* such as a rectangle, and assign a thick stroke to it.

5 Get the Scissors tool and click on a corner point.

The notch that appears is a visual clue that the corner is now made of two separate, unjoined end points. With the white Direct Selection tool, click on the end point to select it, then drag the point to the left (*or* use the arrow keys to nudge the end point to the left).

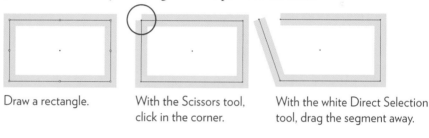

Draw a rectangle.   With the Scissors tool, click in the corner.   With the white Direct Selection tool, drag the segment away.

TASK 16   Use the Knife tool to modify a shape

The Knife tool cuts through objects and paths to create separate objects.

1 With the Ellipse tool, draw a circle. Fill it with a color.

2 With the Knife tool, drag a wavy path across the top section of the circle (below, left). Drag another wavy path across the bottom section of the circle.

3 With the black Selection tool, select each section in turn and assign a different fill color to each (below, center).

4 Create a color variation by filling each section with a gradient from the Swatches panel.

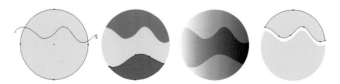

The sections created with the Knife tool are separate shapes that can be modified independently or moved, as shown on the far-right.

Use an envelope to warp objects

An *envelope* is a grid that fits around a selected object (including type) and warps the shape of the object, according to your settings. You can apply preset warp shapes, or customize the warp using the points and handles of the envelope grid.

TASK 17 Warp a type object using a preset warp

1 With the Type tool, type something like "SnakeByte."

SnakeByte

2 Select the type, then choose Object > Envelope Distort > Make with Warp….

3 In the "Warp Options" dialog box that opens, click "Preview," then choose "Flag" from the "Style" pop-up menu.

Below is a preview of the warp with the settings shown to the left.

4 Drag the "Bend" slider to set the amount of warp applied to the type.

The "Distortion" sliders create horizontal and vertical distortion that might (or might not) enhance the effect you want. Try it.

5 Click OK.

The envelope grid is editable: Use the white Direct Selection tool to select one or more points, then drag to another position.

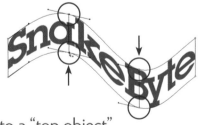

TASK 18 Warp a type object into a "top object"

1 Draw an ellipse and position it on top of the "SnakeByte" type.

2 Marquee around both objects to select them.

3 Choose Object > Envelope Distort > Make with Top Object.

Any fill that was in the ellipse is deleted in the process.

TASK 19   Warp an object using a mesh

1   Select an object. I drew the simple shape below with the Pen tool, then filled it with a preset radial gradient (see pages 161–165).

2   With the object selected, choose Object > Envelope Distort > Make with Mesh….

3   In the "Envelope Mesh" dialog that opens (shown below), set how many rows and columns to include in the mesh. Fewer rows and columns create smoother warping. Click OK.

4   With the white Direct Selection tool, first click off to the side, then click on the object to get editable points. Drag mesh points, handles, or mesh path segments to warp the object. You can also drag anywhere within the mesh, not just on paths and anchor points.

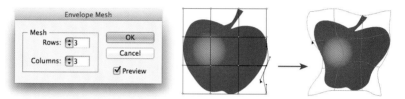

 5   **To add rows and columns to the mesh,** get the Mesh tool (left) from the Tools panel and click in the grid.

   To delete an anchor point on the grid, select it with the white Direct Selection tool (or the Mesh tool), then press Delete (PC: Backspace).

6   **To modify the envelope mesh,** use the black Selection tool to select the mesh, then use the options in the Control panel (shown below).

   To edit the envelope contents, click the "Edit Contents" button.

   To edit the envelope, click the "Edit Envelope" button.

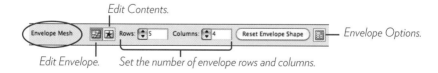

   Expand an envelope so you can work with the new shape: Choose Object > Envelope Distort > Expand. The envelope is deleted, but the warped object has the new control points on it.

   To release the envelope and get the original shape back: Choose Object > Envelope Distort > Release. Two objects are created: the envelope shape and the original, unaltered artwork. Click outside the object, then select the envelope with the black Selection tool and delete it.

181

Pathfinder effects to transform objects

Pathfinder effects let you combine overlapping objects into new shapes, using ten different interaction shape modes.

The Pathfinder panel

To open the Pathfinder panel, choose Window > Pathfinder.

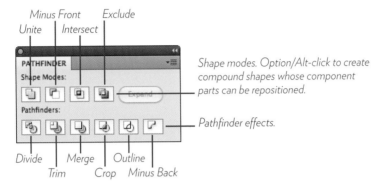

Minus Front   Exclude
Unite   Intersect

Shape modes. Option/Alt-click to create compound shapes whose component parts can be repositioned.

Pathfinder effects.

Divide   Merge   Outline
Trim   Crop   Minus Back

The Shape Mode tools on the top row convert selected overlapping objects into *paths* or *compound paths*. The new shape that's created is one shape; you cannot reposition any former parts because the individual pieces are gone.

To create Shape Mode shapes that you *can* reposition, hold down the Option key (PC: Alt key) when you click one of the Shape Mode buttons. This lets you select one of the component shapes with the Direct Selection tool and reposition it, while still retaining the Pathfinder effect.

TASK 20   Unite two shapes into one shape

1   Draw two shapes that are similar to the ones below-left; overlap them. **Make a copy** so you can do all of the following tasks without having to redraw the original shapes each time!

2   Marquee around the two shapes to select them both.

3   In the Pathfinder panel, click the *Unite* button. The two objects are combined into one (below, right), and the fill and stroke of the top object take over.

TASK 21   Unite two shapes as compound shapes

1   Select the original two shapes again.

2   Option-click (PC: Alt-click) the *Unite* button in the Pathfinder panel.

The two shapes are joined into one, but the original components are still intact. The fill and stroke attributes from the top object take over.

3   With the white Direct Selection tool, drag the star-shaped component to the opposite side of the circle (or anywhere nearby). You can separate them completely, and then when you touch them together again, they remember they are united. Freaky.

This flexible method of combining shapes is a great way to **experiment** with shape interactions. Try it with all of the Shape Mode options on the top row of the Pathfinder panel.

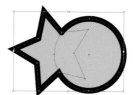 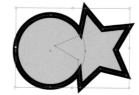

TASK 22   Subtract one shape from another

1   Select the original two shapes again. Select the circle and bring it to the front: Choose Object > Arrange > Bring to Front (below, left).

2   Click the *Minus Front* button in the Pathfinder panel. The star shape is now *minus* the circle shape that was in front (below, center).

3   Now try a variation of this: Undo Step 2 (choose Edit > Undo Subtract). Make sure both shapes are selected, then Option-click (PC: Alt-click) the *Minus Front* button. The appearance is the same, except now the circle *path* is still present and you can reposition it, as shown below-right.

TASK 23   Experiment with the other Pathfinder options

Select the original two shapes. Click the other Pathfinder buttons to see what effects they have on multiple, overlapping objects.

Align and distribute objects

The Align panel lines up and evenly distributes objects horizontally or vertically. Experiment with all of the options so you know what is possible.

TASK 24   Align and distribute objects *by selection*

1   Draw four objects, and space them unevenly, like the ones below.

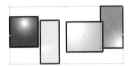

Notice that the center marks in these shapes are not lined up with each other.

2   Use the black Selection tool to select all the objects.

3   Open the Align panel: Choose Window > Align.

4   Click the "Align To" button (shown below), and choose the option to "Align to Selection."

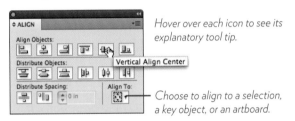

Hover over each icon to see its explanatory tool tip.

Choose to align to a selection, a key object, or an artboard.

5   Click the *Vertical Align Center* button in the "Align Objects" row (shown above). The objects move so their *centers* are aligned vertically.

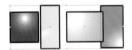

You might think these are aligned horizontally, but actually the center points are all aligned at the same point of a vertical axis.

6   Now click the *Horizontal Distribute Center* button in the "Distribute Objects" row (use the tool tips to find it). The objects' *centers* are evenly distributed, as shown below. See the captions below for other options.

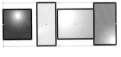

*These objects are aligned vertically by their centers, and the space between them is distributed horizontally **between their centers**. But because they are different widths, the empty space between them is uneven.*

I want the space between the objects to be equally distributed, so I click the Horizontal Distribute Space button (one of the bottom-left buttons).

I also chose → Vertical Align Top.

*The space gets distributed **between the first and last objects**. So put the first and last objects into position, then click to distribute the space. The first and last objects stay in their positions and the other objects are aligned between.*

TASK 25 Distribute space around a *key object*

For more control over the distribution of spacing, align to a **key object**, which is an object in the collection that you choose to arrange the others around.

1 Arrange four objects in a random order, then select all four objects.

2 In the Align panel (shown below), click the *Vertical Align Top* button.

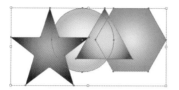

No matter how randomly you had positioned the elements, they are now aligned across their tops.

3 Now you need to select the **key object**. First, in the Align panel, click the "Align To" button; choose "Align to Key Object."

4 Now click to select the object *around which you want to distribute the space* (the circle, for example, as shown below). A bold outline appears around the selected **key object**.

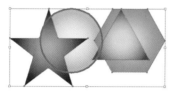

5 In the "Distribute Spacing" field, enter the amount of space you want between all objects, such as 12 pt.

6 Click the *Horizontal Distribute Space* button.

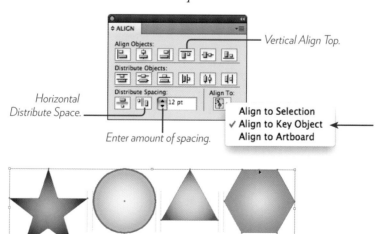

Horizontal Distribute Space.

Enter amount of spacing.

Vertical Align Top.

Align to Selection
✓ Align to Key Object
Align to Artboard

All objects are now separated from each other by 12 points, the amount between the key object and its neighbors. (In this example, the various shapes create an optical illusion of varying amounts of space. But as you can see by the dotted lines, the outermost edge of each object is separated by 12 points.)

The Appearance Panel

Working in the Appearance panel is the same as jumping back and forth between the Color, Swatches, Stroke, and Transparency panels—the controls in all those panels are accessible here. Appearance attributes are those characteristics (such as fills, strokes, graphic styles, and effects) that affect the *appearance* of an object without changing its underlying structure.

When an object is selected, its appearance attributes show up in the Appearance panel, enabling you to edit, remove, or add attributes.

To open the Appearance panel (below), choose Window > Appearance.

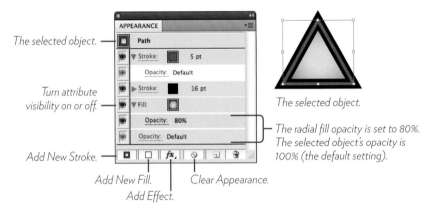

The selected object.

Turn attribute visibility on or off.

Add New Stroke.

Add New Fill.

Add Effect.

Clear Appearance.

The selected object.

The radial fill opacity is set to 80%. The selected object's opacity is 100% (the default setting).

TASK 26 Change the fill and stroke of an object

1 With the Star tool, draw a star with a black color fill and no stroke.

2 In the Appearance panel, click the Fill color swatch (shown below). In the Swatches panel that pops up, choose a fill color *or* a gradient.

3 Click the Stroke swatch to select a stroke color. A stroke weight field also appears; enter an amount, such as 6 pt.

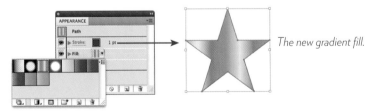

The new gradient fill.

TIP: To make the thumbnails larger, go to the panel menu and choose "Large Thumbnail View."

4   Change the stroke again, in preparation for Task 27: Click the Stroke swatch in the panel; assign a 14-point purple stroke.

For more stroke options, *click the underlined word "Stroke" to open a pop-up version of the full Stroke panel and all its options.*

TASK 27   Add a stroke on top of another stroke

You can add a second stroke to an object; the second stroke is *on top of* the existing stroke, centered within it, which makes it look like three strokes.

1   Select the star you created in the previous step, the one with a heavy stroke. Click the *Add New Stroke* button at the bottom of the panel.

2   Assign a green color and a stroke weight of 4 points to the new stroke.

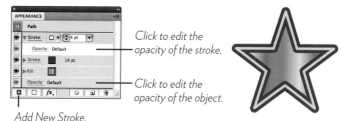

Click to edit the opacity of the stroke.

Click to edit the opacity of the object.

Add New Stroke.

TASK 28   Add an effect

1   Make sure the star is still selected; click the *Add Effect* button at the bottom of the panel.

2   From the pop-up menu that opens, choose Stylize > Scribble.

In the "Scribble Options" dialog box that opens, check "Preview," then experiment with the various settings.

To edit settings, *click an underlined word. Each item has an "Opacity" attribute; the default opacity setting is 100%. If the percentage is changed, the amount appears next to "Opacity."*

Add Effect.

I applied a scribble effect to the green stroke.

Try this!

Use the techniques you learned in this chapter to create a colorful montage of shapes and type. Explore options and settings in the various panels that weren't covered in this chapter. Rotate, reflect, shear, warp, mesh, align, and distribute to your heart's content.

A star shape, filled with a radial gradient.

Knife tool used to cut a curve through the star shape (fill gradient automatically refilled new shapes that were created).

Blending Mode in Transparency panel set to "Multiply."

Arc effect applied to type:
Effect > Warp > Arc.

Blending Mode in Transparency panel set to "Difference."

Small stars:
Filled with radial gradient.

Scribble effect applied:
Effect > Stylize > Scribble.

A circle filled with radial gradient.

Blending Mode in Transparency panel set to "Difference."

A spiky circle:
A circle filled with radial gradient.

Zig Zag effect applied:
Effect > Distort & Transform > Zig Zag.

A dashed line circle:
In the Stroke panel, a fill of None and a Dashed Line stroke applied.

Stroke opacity: 50%.

Stroke Blending Mode in Transparency panel set to "Difference."

13 Shape, Blend, and Mesh

In this chapter you'll learn how to use the Shape Builder tool, an interactive tool that creates new shapes from overlapping shapes—it acts like a Pathfinder panel (Chapter 12) built into a brush. It also acts as a paint bucket to color areas and strokes of shapes.

And you'll love the Blend tool. It blends the color *and* shape of two or more objects.

You won't be able to live without the Mesh tool, which creates objects with sophisticated and complex color shading.

You'll also learn about (and love) Graphic Styles, a convenient time-saving feature that applies collections of settings and effects to an object all in one fell swoop.

The Shape Builder tool

Double-click the Shape Builder tool in the Tools panel to open the "Shape Builder Tool Options" dialog box. You can easily create complex shapes without having to draw them with the Pen tool, plus apply different colors to overlapping areas that might be hard to select otherwise. Read the basic information below, and then follow the tasks to get an idea of the possibilities for future use.

Gap Detection: The Shape Builder tool can detect the gaps between closed objects and in open paths, and then treat the gaps as a *region* (an area) that can be filled with color.

The "Gap Length" (Small, Medium, or Large) determines what size a gap has to be before it's considered a *region.* You can also check the "Custom" box and enter a specific space size.

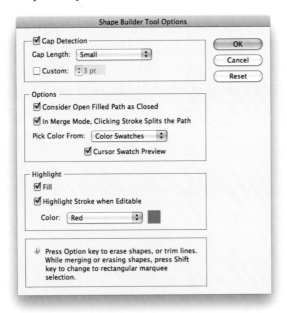

Consider Open Filled Path as Closed: This option creates an invisible edge that closes open paths *and* the space between shapes (shown below). Although Illustrator allows you to fill open or closed paths with color, the Shape Builder tool fills *regions,* and only recognizes *closed* shapes (or spaces) as regions.

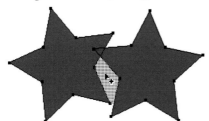

*Because this option is turned on, the Shape Builder tool recognizes the space between the two stars as a **region** and highlights it in gray.*

In Merge Mode, Clicking Stroke Splits the Path: This option enables you to split the parent path into two paths with a click so you can edit them separately.

Pick Color From: You can choose "Color Swatches" or "Artwork." This setting determines the source of colors available for selecting and applying.

> TRY THIS: Select the "Color Swatches" option, as mentioned above, then check the "Cursor Swatch Preview" box. This creates a special pointer that lets you preview and select colors within the pointer.
>
> **Cursor Swatch Preview:**
> The **middle** color swatch is the currently selected color.
> The colors on the **left and right** are the colors that appear on either side of the current color in the Swatches panel.
> **To cycle through colors in the Swatches panel**, tap the left or right arrow keys.

Fill: This highlights regions in gray when the Shape Builder tool hovers over them. Until you get used to the Shape Builder tool behavior, it's best to keep this option turned on so you get the visual feedback.

Highlight Stroke When Editable: This provides helpful visual feedback that tells you which strokes can be edited. Editable strokes will highlight in the color you choose from the "Color" pop-up menu.

TASK 1   Merge regions

1   Draw two simple shapes and give each a different fill and stroke color.

2   With the black Selection tool, select both shapes (below, left).

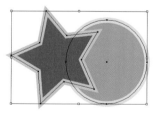

Select the objects that you want to interact with each other.

Regions highlight in gray when the pointer hovers over them.

3   Choose the Shape Builder tool in the Tools panel.

4   Move the pointer over the selected shapes (above, right).

As the pointer moves over the shapes, the *regions* created by the intersection of shapes are highlighted in gray.

—*continued*

5 **To merge the two regions into one**, drag from one region to another (below, center). The regions that are about to be merged are highlighted.

6 Let go to see the results (below, right).

By default, the Shape Builder tool is in Merge mode, indicated by the plus symbol in the pointer.

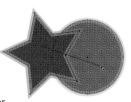 

TASK 2   Color the shape's stroke segments

1 Use the merged version of the shape in Task 1, shown above, right.

2 With the black Selection tool, select the shape.

3 Choose the Shape Builder tool and hover the pointer over the stroke (below, left). The path highlights in red (or whatever color you chose as a highlight color in the dialog box shown on page 190).

4 Tap the arrow keys until the stroke color you want appears in the middle preview color box in the pointer (below, left), then click (below, right).

Or choose a color swatch in the Swatches panel.

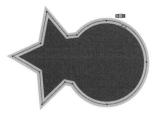 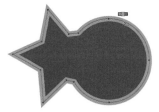

Hover over a path and the pointer changes to a stroke color tool.

Click the path to assign the current path color to the highlighted path.

TASK 3 Delete a region

1   Select two overlapping shapes.

2   With the Shape Builder tool, hover the pointer over the region you want to delete (below, center).

3   Option-click (PC: Alt-click) the region. This deletes the targeted region, creating a compound path (a shape with a hole in it).

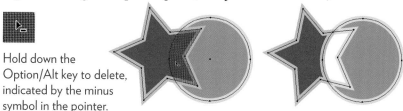

Hold down the Option/Alt key to delete, indicated by the minus symbol in the pointer.

TASK 4 Color the regions

1   Select the two overlapping shapes as they appear at the end of Task 3.

2   Choose the Shape Builder tool, then hover the pointer over a region to highlight it (below, left).

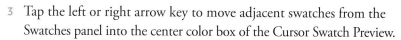

With the Cursor Swatch Preview turned on (page 191), the current Fill color appears in the middle color box in the pointer.

3   Tap the left or right arrow key to move adjacent swatches from the Swatches panel into the center color box of the Cursor Swatch Preview.

4   When the color you want is in the pointer's middle preview box (below, left), click the region you want to color (*or* choose a color directly from the Swatches panel to apply it, as usual).

Hover over the region you want to fill with color.

Click to fill the region with the selected color.

TIP: There can be so many color swatches in the Swatches panel that it's inconvenient to cycle through them. In the Swatches panel, drag the colors you want to work with to arrange them next to each other so they will be just a tap or two away.

Blend paths, shapes, and colors

The Blend tool blends two or more objects (paths or shapes), creating a blend of both color *and* shape. When you create a blend, you can choose one of three different "Spacing" methods: *Smooth Color, Specified Steps* (the number of steps in the blend), or *Specified Distance* (the distance between corresponding edges of blend steps).

A "Smooth Color" blend of two paths.   A "Specified Steps" blend of two shapes.

The Blend Options dialog box

To open the Blend Options dialog box, double-click the Blend tool.

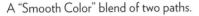

When you want to choose a spacing method for the blend, use the "Spacing" pop-up menu.

The "Orientation" option determines the orientation of blended objects: perpendicular to the *page* or perpendicular to the blend *spine* (the blend's path, as shown on page 197). This orientation is noticeable if the blend spine is curved.

TASK 5   Blend two open paths with smooth color

1   Use the Pen tool to draw an open path (shown below).

2   Create a duplicate of the path: Option-drag (PC: Alt-drag) the path to a position just below the original.

3   Assign each stroke a different color. The path in this example has a heavy stroke for visibility on the page, but it can be any weight.

4 Double-click the Blend tool in the Tools panel; select "Smooth Color" from the "Spacing" pop-up menu. Click OK.

5 With the Blend tool, click the path of one stroke, then click the path of the second stroke. (Notice that the strokes don't have to be selected before you click them with the Blend tool.)

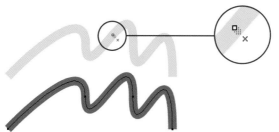

When the Blend tool is positioned exactly over the path, the pointer changes to include an X symbol.

6 The results of the blend are shown below. NOTE: You can still select the top or bottom stroke with the white Direct Selection tool, then move or reshape the paths, or assign a different stroke color!

TASK 6 Blend two paths with a specified number of steps

1 Draw an open path, then create a duplicate, as in Task 5. Assign a different color stroke to each path.

2 Drag the bottom stroke farther away from the top stroke (to make room for blended objects in Step 5).

3 Double-click the Blend tool; from the "Spacing" pop-up menu, choose "Specified Steps."

4 In the "Specified Steps" field, type "3." Click OK.

5 With the Blend tool, click the path of one stroke, then click the path of the second stroke.

The two strokes that are to be blended.   The blended strokes.

TASK 7 Blend two shapes with smooth color

1   Draw two star shapes of different sizes, then space them a distance apart, as shown below.

2   Assign a different fill color for each shape.

3   Double-click the Blend tool to open the "Blend Options" dialog box; from the "Spacing" pop-up menu, select "Smooth Color."

4   Choose the Blend tool; click one shape, then click the other shape.

You can still select either star with the white Direct Selection tool, then move the shape or assign a different fill color!

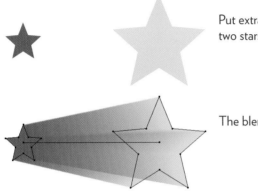

Put extra space between the two stars that are to be blended.

The blend results.

TASK 8 Blend two shapes with a specified number of steps

1   Draw two star shapes of different sizes, then space them a distance apart, as shown above.

2   Assign a different fill color to each shape.

3   Double-click the Blend tool to open the "Blend Options" dialog box; from the "Spacing" pop-up menu, choose "Specified Steps."

4   Enter "10" into the "Specified Steps" field.

5   Choose the Blend tool; click one shape, then click the other shape.

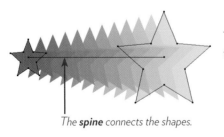

Two stars blended with ten blending steps.

The **spine** connects the shapes.

TASK 9 Modify the blend spine

1   With the white Direct Selection tool, select the *spine* (the path that now connects the shapes) of the blended objects in Task 8.

2   With the Pen tool, click on the spine to add a new anchor point. If you want, click again in another spot to create a second anchor point.

3   With the Convert Anchor Point tool (hidden under the Pen tool), drag handles out of the points to convert them to smooth points.

4   With the white Direct Selection tool, drag the smooth points to new positions. Drag the direction handles to modify the spine curves.

You can also select either end object with the white Direct Selection tool, then change its color fill.

5   Experiment with gradient fills: Assign different gradient fills to the two end objects, as explained on pages 155–159. Try both linear gradients and radial gradients.

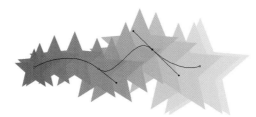

Modify the curved spine as you would any path.

TASK 10 Modify the blend's stroke size and color

1   Using the blended shapes you created in Task 9, select the star shape on the *left* side of the blend (the end object).

2   Change the stroke color and weight of the star. Use either the Stroke options in the Control panel or the Stroke panel.

3   Select the other star shape on the *right* side of the blend and change its stroke attributes.

The star shape on the left has a 3-point gold stroke; the star on the right has a 10-point purple stroke.

TASK 11   Replace the blend's spine with another path

1   Draw two small star shapes of the same or similar size, then space them a distance apart, as shown below.

2   Assign a different fill color to each shape.

3   To open the "Blend Options" dialog box, double-click the Blend tool. From the "Spacing" pop-up menu, choose "Specified Distance." In the "Specified Distance" field, enter "50 pt." (You may need to use a different "Specified Distance" value, depending on the size of your star shapes and the distance between them.)

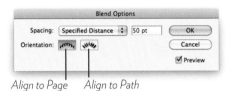

Align to Page   Align to Path

4   With the Blend tool, click one star shape, then click the other star shape to create the blend shown below.

5   On another part of the artboard, draw a path to use as the new spine (below, left), *or* select an existing path that you want to use.

6   With the black Selection tool, select both the blended object (the stars) *and* the path that is to replace the spine of the blended object.

7   Choose Object > Blend > Replace Spine. The result of the spine replacement is shown below, right.

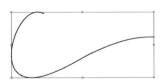   

I drew this path with the Pencil tool.   *The blended object follows the path of*
The stroke weight is not important   *the replacement spine!*
because only the path will be used.

8   Also try changing the blend orientation: Double-click the Blend tool. In the "Blend Options" dialog box (shown above), click the *Align to Path* button. You can also change the "Specified Distance" value.

TASK 12   Create a blend using the Blend command

You can also create blends by using the Blend command in the Object menu. And instead of double-clicking the Blend tool to open the "Blend Options" dialog box, you can choose Object > Blend > Blend Options….

1   Select the objects you want to blend.

2   Choose Object > Blend > Make.

TASK 13   Reverse the stacking order of a blend

1   Select the blend.

2   Choose Object > Blend > Reverse Front to Back.

The original blend.   *The blend with the stacking order reversed.*

TASK 14   Reverse a blend

1   Select the blended object.

2   Choose Object > Blend > Reverse Spine.

The original blend.   *The blend with the spine reversed.*

TASK 15   Release a blended object

When you release a blended object, the blend steps are removed, leaving intact the original objects that were used to make the blend.

1   Select the blended object.

2   Choose Object > Blend > Release.

TASK 16   Expand a blended object

When you expand a blended object, each step of the blend is converted to paths and the editable spine is deleted.

1   Select the blended object.

2   Choose Object > Blend > Expand.

Amazing mesh objects

A **mesh object** is a vector shape covered with a grid of mesh lines that enables you to fill the shape with different colors, almost as if you were using the airbrush tool in Photoshop.

The Mesh tool lets you create multiple gradients that blend into each other.

The Mesh tool lets you control the transitions of color and shading.

TASK 17   Create a Gradient Mesh object

Follow along for the next four tasks to create the apple shown above. This will make you comfortable with the way mesh objects work.

1   Draw a circle, then choose a fill color of blue (below, left).

2   Choose Object > Create Gradient Mesh….

3   In the "Create Gradient Mesh" dialog box that opens (shown below), click "Preview," then set the number of "Rows" and "Columns" to "3" (using only a few rows and columns results in smoother gradients).

4   Click the "Appearance" pop-up menu and choose "To Center." This automatically creates a white highlight in the middle of the object.

5   Set the "Highlight" value (the white highlight) to 100%. Click OK.

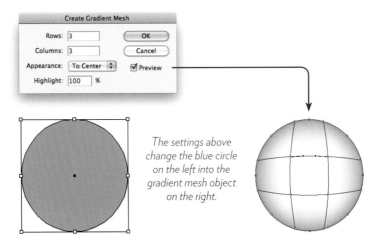

The settings above change the blue circle on the left into the gradient mesh object on the right.

Overview of a mesh object

A mesh object is made up of the components shown below.

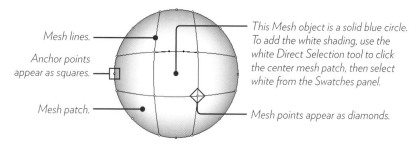

Mesh lines.

Anchor points appear as squares.

Mesh patch.

This Mesh object is a solid blue circle. To add the white shading, use the white Direct Selection tool to click the center mesh patch, then select white from the Swatches panel.

Mesh points appear as diamonds.

Mesh lines: Horizontal and vertical lines create a grid on top of the object.

Mesh patch: The area between mesh lines. When you add color to a mesh *patch,* the color spreads out more than when you add color to a mesh *point.*

Drag a mesh patch to nudge the surrounding color blends.

Mesh point: Mesh points appear as diamonds at points where mesh lines intersect. Use them to add color to the mesh or to nudge the color around.

Color assigned to mesh points and patches blends into surrounding colors.

To change the appearance of the color blends in the mesh, use the white Direct Selection tool. Move mesh points or drag mesh point handles to modify the curves (which also affects the appearance of the color blends).

Anchor point: Anchor points appear as squares and make up the basic structure of the object. You can move them with the white Direct Selection tool to influence the flow of the color gradient, but they can't be filled with color as a mesh point can.

TASK 18   Using the Mesh tool

Use the Mesh tool to add or remove mesh lines or mesh points, as well as to add colors to the mesh.

1   **Add a new mesh point to a mesh line.** With the Mesh tool, click a mesh line. When you hover over a mesh line, the pointer displays a plus symbol to indicate a new mesh point will be added at that point.

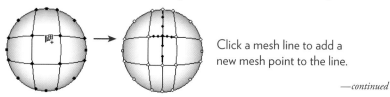

Click a mesh line to add a new mesh point to the line.

—continued

2 **Remove a mesh line or a mesh point.** Option-click (PC: Alt-click) a mesh line or mesh point with the Mesh tool. The pointer displays a minus symbol to indicate the line or point will be deleted (below).

Option-click (PC: Alt-click) a mesh line or mesh point to remove it.

3 **Add a new mesh point with horizontal and vertical mesh lines to the mesh grid.** Click a mesh *patch* (the space between mesh lines). When the pointer is hovered over a mesh patch, it displays a plus symbol to indicate a new mesh point, and mesh lines will be added at that point.

Click a mesh patch to add to the mesh grid.

4 **Add color to a mesh point.** With the Mesh tool (*or* with the white Direct Selection tool), click a mesh point (below, left), then select a color from the Swatches panel, Control panel, or Color panel.

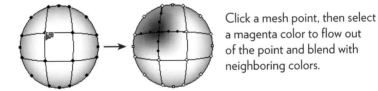

Click a mesh point, then select a magenta color to flow out of the point and blend with neighboring colors.

5 **Add color to a mesh patch.** With the white Direct Selection tool, click a mesh patch (below, left).

Don't use the Mesh tool to select a mesh patch. When you click inside a mesh patch with the Mesh tool, it creates a new mesh point instead of selecting the mesh patch.

When a mesh patch is selected, all the surrounding mesh points are also selected; choose a color from the Swatches panel, Control panel, or Color panel (below, right).

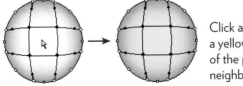

Click a mesh patch, then select a yellow color to flow out of the patch and blend with neighboring colors.

TASK 19   Create a colorful, circular, gradient mesh object

1   Draw a circle and convert it to a gradient mesh object, as described in Task 17.

2   With the Mesh tool *or* the white Direct Selection tool, select the mesh points on the *left* side of the object. Then choose a purple color from the Swatches panel.

3   In the same manner, select the mesh points on the *right* side of the object, then choose a green color from the Swatches panel.

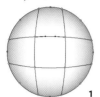
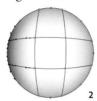
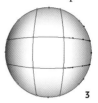

4   With the white Direct Selection tool, click the center mesh patch; choose a yellow color from the Swatches panel.

5   With the white Direct Selection tool, drag the center mesh patch to the left to nudge colors in that direction.

6   With the Mesh tool (*or* the white Direct Selection tool), click the top-left mesh line intersection; select the white swatch from the Swatches panel to create a highlight.

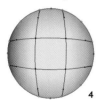
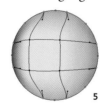

7   With the white Direct Selection tool, click the top two mesh points; choose a dark blue color from the Swatches panel.

With the white Direct Selection tool, adjust the top and bottom handles of the vertical mesh lines to smooth the curves a bit.

8   The final gradient mesh—more versatile than ordinary gradients.

TASK 20 Create an apple from a circular mesh object

1 **Draw a circle:** Fill the circle with red and convert it to a gradient mesh object, as described in Task 17, Steps 1–3.

2 Choose Object > Create Gradient Mesh….
In the dialog box that opens, click the "Appearance" menu and choose "Flat." The mesh object fills with a flat red color. Click OK.

3 **Create a highlight:** With the white Direct Selection tool, click the top-left mesh intersection; choose the white swatch from the Swatches panel. The white highlight color flows from the mesh point intersection to the surrounding area.

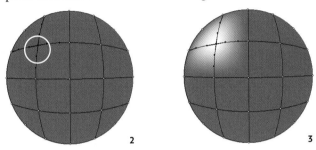

4 **Shade the right side of the object:** With the white Direct Selection tool, select all of the mesh points on the *right* side of the circle; from the Swatches panel, select a darker red.

5 **Adjust the shading:** With the Mesh tool, click the center mesh line near the bottom of the circle to create a new horizontal mesh line.

With the white Direct Selection tool, click that new mesh intersection point (where the center mesh line crosses the new horizontal mesh line) to select it.

Choose the original bright red color to cover up some of the dark red shading at the bottom of the circle.

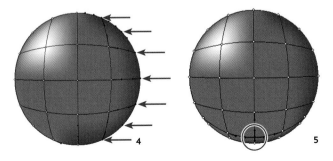

6 **Create a reflected highlight:** With the white Direct Selection tool, select the mesh points on the vertical mesh line to the right of the center mesh line (circled, below-left).

With the points selected, choose a lighter tint of the original red color to add the appearance of soft, reflected light on the shadow side of the object (the right side).

7 **Distort the object to be more apple-like:** With the white Direct Selection tool, select the lower-outside points on the *left* side of the object, then use the right arrow key to nudge the shape inward toward the center.

Select the corresponding points on the *right* side and use the left Arrow key to nudge them to the left, inward toward the center.

Select the top-center point; nudge it downward with the down arrow key.

Select the two bottom-center points; nudge them upward with the up arrow key.

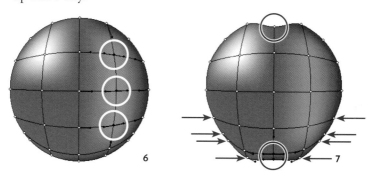

8 **Create a top highlight area:** With the Mesh tool, click on the center vertical mesh line, just below the top of the object, to create a new mesh line (below). Drag the mesh point handles to curve the new mesh line.

Click again to create a second mesh line, just above and very close to the first one, as shown below (close mesh lines create sudden color transitions and harder edges). Select the first mesh line (the lower one), then choose a light tint of red to create a soft highlight.

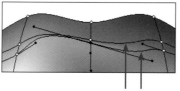

Two new mesh lines.

Move mesh lines close together to create harder edges. The mesh line above the selected mesh line is there just to stop the highlight color from blending to the edge of the object.

—continued

9 **Create an additional vertical highlight on the left side** to prevent gradient color from getting too close to the edge of the object: With the Mesh tool, click on the existing center horizontal mesh line, close to the left edge (see the closeup below, left); this creates a new vertical mesh line.

10 **Create another vertical mesh line** on which to create a color highlight: Click again on the same horizontal mesh line as in the previous step, but click a little to the *right* of the previous click.

11 **Add color to this new highlight mesh line:** Select the three mesh points near the center of this vertical mesh line (circled, below-right), then choose a light yellow color from the Swatches panel.

Drag these two mesh lines close together. See Step 8.

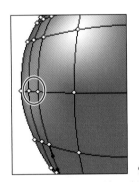

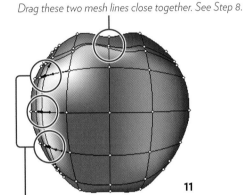

9–10

Create two new vertical mesh lines. Click this horizontal mesh line at these two points.

11

Select these three mesh points, then select a light yellow color.

12 **This is the finished apple.** I added an apple stem, a simple shape drawn with the Pen tool and filled with a linear gradient.

12

Keep experimenting.

Drag mesh patches, mesh points, and mesh handles to different positions to see how they affect the gradients.

Select mesh paths and mesh points, then choose different colors for them.

Draw different shapes and practice amazing mesh stuff.

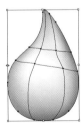

Graphic styles

A **graphic style** is a collection of appearance attributes that you can apply all at once to objects. For example, let's say you format an object with a fill color, a stroke weight and color, an opacity setting, and an effect; you can save those settings as a graphic style that can be applied later to other objects.

You can apply graphic styles to objects, groups, or layers. If you target a layer and apply a graphic style, all objects on that layer take on the appearance of the graphic style. *If you move an object out of that layer to another layer, the object no longer shows the effects of the layer's graphic style.*

The Graphic Styles panel

To open the Graphic Styles panel, choose Window > Graphic Styles. When you first open the panel, there are just a few graphic style thumbnails in the panel. You can add others from graphic styles libraries, or create your own custom styles.

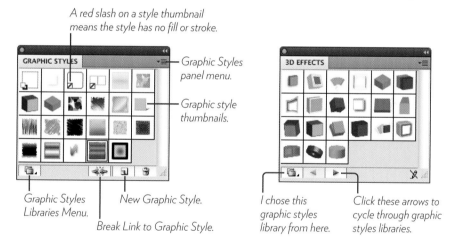

A red slash on a style thumbnail means the style has no fill or stroke.

Graphic Styles panel menu.

Graphic style thumbnails.

Graphic Styles Libraries Menu.

New Graphic Style.

Break Link to Graphic Style.

I chose this graphic styles library from here.

Click these arrows to cycle through graphic styles libraries.

TASK 21   Open a Graphic Styles library

1   Open the Graphic Styles panel.

2   Click the *Graphic Styles Libraries Menu* button in the bottom-left corner of the panel to pop up a list of libraries.

3   From the list, choose "3D Effects"; this opens the "3D Effects" panel shown above, right.

4   Click a thumbnail to apply the style to a selected object.

TASK 22   Add a graphic style to the Graphic Styles panel

1   Open a Graphic Styles library panel (see Task 21).

2   Click a Graphic Styles thumbnail. This automatically adds that style to the Graphic Styles panel. If an object is selected, the style is *also* applied to the selection.

TASK 23   Preview graphic styles

A generic preview is shown in each style's thumbnail.

To see a larger thumbnail preview that's based on a *selection,* hold down the Control key and *press* on a style thumbnail. A preview appears to display the style applied to the selected object.

To show a custom preview, first select an object on the page. Then Control-press on a thumbnail.

TASK 24   Create a custom graphic style

A custom style doesn't have to be fancy to be useful. Create custom styles for any formatting that you use a lot. It's a great timesaver.

1   Draw a 7-point star, as shown below. Choose a fill color of red.

2   Assign the star a stroke weight of 12 points and a stroke color of gold (below, left).

3   Drag the object into the Graphic Styles panel.

4   To name your custom style, double-click the new thumbnail.

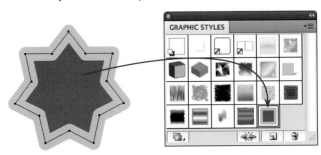

TASK 25   Edit graphic styles that are applied to an object

1   Apply a graphic style to an object: Select the 7-point star you created in Task 24, then apply a style from the Graphic Styles panel.

If your Graphic Styles panel is still sparse, click the *Graphic Styles Libraries Menu* button in the bottom-left corner, choose "Scribble Effects," then click the *Scribble 2* thumbnail to add it to the Graphic Styles panel (as shown below).

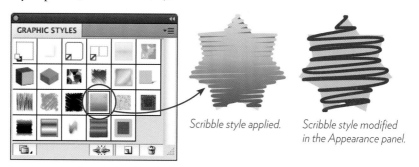

Scribble style applied.   *Scribble style modified in the Appearance panel.*

2   With the star object selected, open the Appearance panel.

This panel provides access to the style's attributes. Click the triangles next to "Stroke" and "Fill" to reveal attribute settings, then change them. The result of the changes I made in the Appearance panel, noted below, are shown above, right.

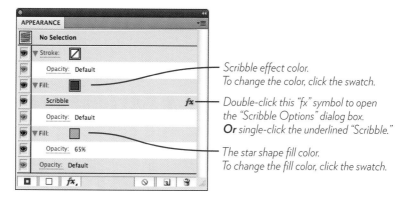

Scribble effect color.
To change the color, click the swatch.

Double-click this "fx" symbol to open the "Scribble Options" dialog box.
***Or** single-click the underlined "Scribble."*

The star shape fill color.
To change the fill color, click the swatch.

Explore more of the Graphic Styles libraries!

There are many great-looking and useful styles tucked away in the libraries. Spend a few minutes to create objects and experiment with more of the options. And don't forget you can modify the styling by making changes in the Appearance panel.

Try this!

Use shape, blend, and mesh techniques to create a colorful graphic. At this point, don't worry too much about the design—become familiar with the tools and techniques so when you start to design, you know how to create on the screen what you see in your mind.

The graphic shown in outline view mode.

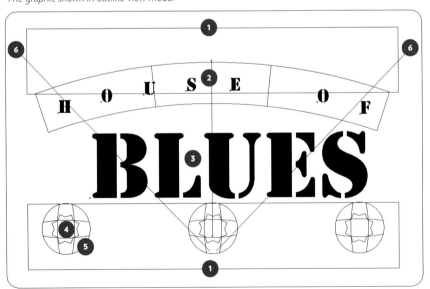

1 Blue and purple rectangles blended together. **2** Green and orange star shapes blended together.
3 Graphic style (3D Effects) applied to text. **4** Star shapes with radial gradient. **5** Gradient mesh object.
6 Yellow and red strokes blended together, using 20 steps.

14 Live Paint and Other Thrills

Illustrator's Live Paint feature not only makes painting shapes and strokes quick and easy, it can also create the illusion of a shape being on top of another shape at one spot, while being behind the same shape at another spot.

This is pretty thrilling stuff to anyone who has spent hours trying to create similar effects in the past, before the Glorious Live Paint Era.

This logo, or device (designed in about 1610 by Mary Sidney Herbert, the Countess of Pembroke), was carved in stone, which was probably more difficult to do than using Live Paint in Illustrator.

Live Paint groups

When you create a Live Paint group, overlapping shapes create *regions* (similar to the regions created by the Path Builder tool). Live Paint treats regions as if they're all on the same level instead of arranged in a stacking order; this is what allows you to overlap areas in a way that appears as if they are weaving in and out of each other on separate layers of the stack.

To work with Live Paint, you must use the **Live Paint Bucket tool** to create a **Live Paint group.** Before you start, set a few options for the Live Paint Bucket tool.

TASK 1   Set the Live Paint Bucket options

1   To open the "Live Paint Bucket Options" dialog box, double-click the Live Paint Bucket tool in the Tools panel (it's grouped with the Shape Builder tool).

2   In the "Options" section, use the settings shown below. This enables the Live Paint Bucket tool to color fills and strokes, and also ensures that the "Cursor Swatch Preview" (shown below, right) is available as you work.

3   In the "Highlight" section, choose a color and width for the highlight stroke that will appear when the Live Paint Bucket tool hovers over any part of a Live Paint group (Live Paint renames what you think of as a stroke or fill as an "edge" or "face").

Depending on the color of the artwork that you're working with, you might want to come here at various times in the process and change the highlight color or width so it's easier to see.

*The **Cursor Swatch Preview** lets you preview adjacent colors in the Swatches panel. **To switch colors,** tap the left or right arrow keys.*

TASK 2 Create a Live Paint group made of shapes

Before you can use Live Paint, you need to turn selected objects into a Live Paint group.

1 Create two or more objects that have different color fills and no strokes, like the shapes below.

2 With the black Selection tool, select the objects.

3 Choose the Live Paint Bucket tool in the Tools panel; click anywhere within the bounding box of the selected group (below, left).

4 With the black Selection tool, select the Live Paint group. Notice the handles of the bounding box now have a different appearance that identifies the group as a Live Paint group (below, right).

Yes, this tiny tool tip appears with the cursor to tell you what to do!

This is an example of the kind of effect you can achieve. If you've ever tried to curl one object both in front of and behind another, you can appreciate how great this is.

TASK 3 Paint overlapping sections for an over/under effect

Live Paint groups treat all paths (called *edges*) and filled shapes (called *faces*) as if they're on the same flat surface, instead of treating some shapes as if they're on top and others as if they're below in a stacking order of objects.

Use the Live Paint Bucket tool to paint overlapping sections with a color that creates the illusion that the *face* is on top of, or below, another shape.

1 Draw two overlapping spirals: With the Spiral tool, draw a spiral; assign it a light blue stroke color.

   Duplicate the spiral: Option-drag (PC: Alt-drag) a copy to the left or right; assign it a red stroke color. Make sure it overlaps the first one.

2 Convert the two stroked paths to shapes (just because we're only dealing with shapes right now): With the black Selection tool, select the two shapes; choose Object > Expand….

   In the "Expand" dialog box that opens, choose to expand the "Stroke," then click OK. The result is shown below, left.

3 With the black Selection tool, select both shapes.

4 With the Live Paint Bucket tool, click the selection to create a Live Paint group (below, right).

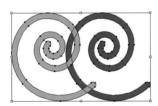 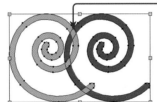

Each of these different segments separated by lines is considered a different **face.**

5 Hover the Live Paint Bucket tool over the top intersecting *face* (shown above, right). The face intersection (shown below, left) highlights with the highlight color you chose in the "Live Paint Bucket Options" dialog box.

   Click on the face to fill it with the current fill color (below, left). Repeat this step on other intersections you want to paint. The final result is shown below, right.

Before click.   *After click.*   *The final over/under effect.*

The **Cursor Swatch Preview** *displays the current fill color in the* **center** *swatch.*

TASK 4 Paint a Live Paint group made of paths

1 With the Pencil tool (or any drawing tool you prefer), assign a 4-point black stroke (depending on the size of your drawing, you may want to assign a different stroke weight).

2 Create a coloring-book-style drawing to paint (below, left).

3 With the black Selection tool, marquee around the drawing so all paths in the drawing are selected.

4 Turn the selection into a Live Paint group: With the Live Paint Bucket tool, click within the bounding box of the selected paths (below, right).

5 Paint the faces of the drawing: Hover the Live Paint Bucket tool over a face (a fill area). The border of the face highlights in the color and weight (below, left) that you chose in Task 1.

Choose a fill color.

6 **Use the Cursor Swatch Preview:** The *Cursor Swatch Preview* that you turned on in Task 1 displays the current fill color in the center box of its icon. When you click a Live Paint face, that color fills the face.

To cycle through the colors in your Swatches panel, tap the left or right arrow keys. When the center box of the Cursor Swatch Preview shows the color you want, click the face.

This lets you move quickly from one face to another, switch colors with a tap or two, then click.

TASK 5 Add paths to a Live Paint group

1 Use the Pencil tool to draw extra paths on the petals of the flower you created in Task 4.

2 With the black Selection tool, select the flower Live Paint group *and* the extra paths you just added.

3 Choose Object > Live Paint > Merge.

4 Choose the Live Paint Bucket tool; hover over the new faces and choose colors in the Cursor Swatch Preview—tap the arrow keys to get the color you want in the center swatch, then click.

New paths.

TASK 6 Paint the paths of a Live Paint group

When you hover the Live Paint Bucket tool over an edge instead of a face, the cursor changes to a brush icon and highlights the edge. Edges in Live Paint groups are broken into segments where other edges meet them.

1 Hover the Live Paint Bucket tool over an edge; you should see a paint brush icon instead of a paint bucket. The edge highlights in the color you chose in Task 1. (If you don't see the paint brush icon, go back to Task 1 and make sure "Paint Strokes" is checked on.)

2 Click the edge with the paint brush cursor to apply the current stroke color (the color in the center box of the Cursor Swatch Preview).

3 To change edge colors in the Cursor Swatch Preview, tap the left or right arrow keys to cycle through adjacent colors in the Swatches panel.

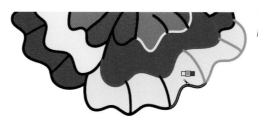

The Live Paint Bucket tool can paint both faces and edges.

> **TIP:** To more quickly select colors with the Cursor Swatch Preview, create a new color group in the Swatches panel that contains the colors you want, then click that color folder to make only those colors appear in the Cursor Swatch Preview.

Work magic with opacity masks

Live Paint works great for simple objects, but sometimes you need to create the same above/below effect with more complex objects. An **opacity mask** lets you hide parts of the artwork to create the illusion that part of it is hidden behind another object. Follow along with this simplified task (see the result in Step 7) so you can apply it to your art when necessary

TASK 7   Create an opaque mask

1   Draw a circle and assign a red fill color to it.

2   Use the Blob brush to draw a gray, snake-like shape on top of the circle.

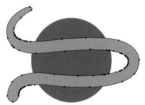

3   With the gray snake-shape selected, open the Transparency panel (Window > Transparency).

Set the snake-shape Opacity to 50%, so you can see the edges of the circle shape through the snake shape.

4   Double-click the blank space next to the snake-shape thumbnail.

Double-click here (see Step 4).

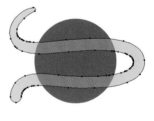

A black outline indicates which element is selected—the artwork (the left thumbnail) or the opacity mask (the right thumbnail).

Make sure the "Clip" and "Invert Mask" items are *not* selected.

The opacity mask thumbnail area.

5 Draw a shape around the part of the snake shape you want to hide: With the opacity mask thumbnail selected, set the fill color to black, then use the Pen tool to draw the shape. Make sure the path you draw matches the circle edges perfectly (the other edges can be more rough). The black-filled path you draw appears in the opacity mask thumbnail.

6 Select the snake-shape thumbnail and reset its opacity to 100%.

The final opacity mask version.   *A similar opacity mask, applied to a more complex example of artwork.*

Mask art with clipping masks

A **clipping mask** is a vector shape that masks artwork in such a way that only areas within the shape area are visible. It's similar to cropping an image, except you can use any shape as a clipping mask, and nothing gets deleted.

TASK 8 Create a clipping mask

1 Draw a shape to use as the *clipping path* (like the star shape below); place that shape on top of the artwork you want to mask.

2 With the black Selection tool, marquee around the artwork *and* the clipping path to select them both (the combination is now called a *clipping set*); choose Object > Clipping Mask > Make.

To see all of the image again, *choose Object > Clipping Mask > Release.*

219

Try this!

Use the Live Paint Bucket tool to create a mysterious blue planet circled by a Saturn-like ring. If you still feel adventurous after this journey through the Illustrator galaxy, add a thick black stroke to the object edges after you create the planet effect.

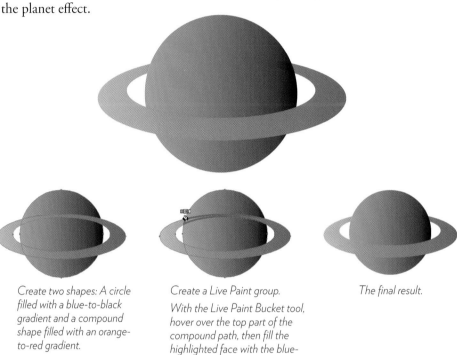

Create two shapes: A circle filled with a blue-to-black gradient and a compound shape filled with an orange-to-red gradient.

Create a Live Paint group.

With the Live Paint Bucket tool, hover over the top part of the compound path, then fill the highlighted face with the blue-to-black gradient.

The final result.

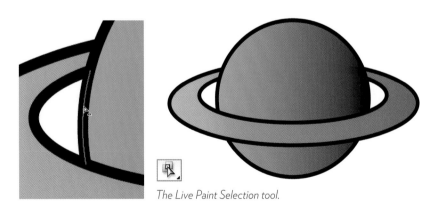

The Live Paint Selection tool.

To add a black stroke: Select the Live Paint Selection tool in the Tools panel (it's grouped with the Live Paint Bucket tool). Hover the cursor over an edge (above left), choose black from the Swatches panel, then assign a stroke weight of 6 points (or whatever weight works for your drawing). Continue to select edges and apply a black stroke.

Index